COACH YOURSELF
SOCCER

Goalkeepers p1

Strikers – p 121

COACH YOURSELF SOCCER

by
ALLEN WADE
Director of Coaching
THE FOOTBALL ASSOCIATION

Photography by MONTE FRESCO

EP Publishing Ltd.
1978

EP Publishing Ltd., Bradford Rd., East Ardsley, Wakefield,
West Yorkshire

First Edition   1970
Reprinted   1971
Reprinted   1972
Limp Edition 1975
Reprinted   1978

I.S.B.N. 0 7158 0177 5

We acknowledge the help and co-operation
which we received from the
CHELSEA FOOTBALL & ATHLETIC CO. LTD.
and in particular
PETER BONETTI, JOHN HOLLINS and PETER OSGOOD
in the preparation of this book.

Printed in Great Britain by
Dixon & Stell Ltd., Cross Hills, nr. Keighley, Yorkshire

GOALKEEPERS

CONTENTS

Football is the greatest game in the world because it has skill, excitement and teamwork. Above all, it is spectacular.

The sight of a forward moving in on goal and casually flicking the ball into the net, or almost bursting the net with a volley taken in mid-air is part of this great spectacle. Goal scoring is spectacular because we know that the apparent certainty of a goal can be denied by a breathtaking save from the goalkeeper.

More than any other player on the field, the goalkeeper carries great responsibilities. Forwards, mid-field players and back defenders can make mistakes which they know they may have a chance to rectify. The striker who misses a goal scoring chance knows that other chances will occur, but the goalkeeper's mistakes are usually final.

The team which is playing well but has an unsafe goal-keeper quickly loses confidence. The poor team with a good, safe goalkeeper grows in confidence with every game.

A goalkeeper must have the skill to catch the ball cleanly, or perhaps turn it round the post or over the bar. He must be able to stop shots from all angles, some of which are powerful and may spin and swerve viciously.

'Shot stopping' is, however, a small part of real goal-keeping skill. Being able to read the game so well that he can anticipate difficulty and stop many shots from being taken is essential. This will enable him to dominate almost all the penalty area, catching high crosses and diving at the feet of a forward who is just about to shoot.

Goalkeepers are the last line of defence, but great goal-keepers are more than that: they are the first line of attack. When they have the ball in their hands they think like a highly skilful, mid-field player and take advantage of any oppor-tunity to instigate an attack with accurate passes (throws and kicks) to the feet of unmarked team-mates. The goal-keeper must 'think' football in exactly the same way as any other player.

It is often said that the spectator sees more of the game than the players. If this is true, then the goalkeeper is in the best position, for long periods during the game, to watch and study all the developments in play.

There is no special size for a goalkeeper. There have been great goalkeepers who were fat, thin and knock-kneed. Some have been big and others have been relatively small, but all have had certain common characteristics.

Courage—he must have the nerve to go into positions where there will be a possibility of hard physical contact in which he will have little chance of protecting himself. Goalkeepers develop skill and experience in going into dangerous situations, but they must be prepared to take hard knocks. There will be many of them.

Confidence—in many situations, he has to react like lightning to make a save. He has only a fraction of time to make a decision about what to do, and having made a decision, must carry it through. Those goalkeepers who are always changing their minds cause their defending players to become unsure. Far better to be decisive and wrong occasionally.

Agility—goalkeeping agility is the ability to put your body in strange positions, often in mid-air, while changing these positions very rapidly indeed.

Strength—agility demands suppleness and strength, since a goalkeeper must resist the possibility of physical challenge while he is in an exposed position. When he goes for a ball he must be prepared to move all other players out of the way by the strength and determination of his jump or dive.

Anticipation—this is really related to the development of an ability to 'read' the game. Good goalkeepers anticipate by knowledge, not by instinct, and this makes great goalkeeping appear simple and totally safe. 'Flashy' goalkeepers are those who are always throwing themselves about at the last moment and who make simple shots look difficult.

Safe and well tried methods are the foundations of goalkeeping skill. Goalkeepers use slightly different methods to suit differences in physical build and height, but these methods will be the result of long practice and will be basically safe.

Positional Play

The situations which a goalkeeper faces change quickly and often he has very few 'cues' from the general development of play. He must adopt positions based upon reasonable probabilities, and be prepared to re-adjust his position as circumstances change.

In figure 1 where an opposing attacker (Black 7) has broken clear with the ball and drawn defenders into bad positions, there are a number of choices open to the goalkeeper.

(a) He can run out and try to get as near to No. 7 as he can before that player shoots. If he does this he knows that No. 7 may chip the ball across the goal for the incoming No. 11 to score a goal.

(b) He can stay in goal, moving across to face the shot, hoping that the nearest back (No. 2) will be able to make a challenge which may put the forward off his shot. He now gives No. 7 a better chance of scoring direct and if No. 7 decides to pass across goal, there is possibly a greater likelihood of No. 11 scoring.

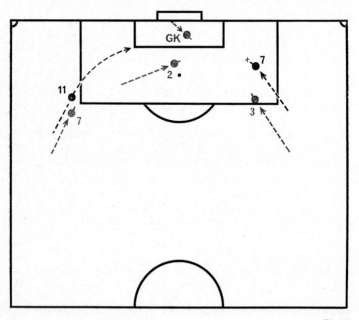

 Fig.1

(c) He can move out, offering a slightly larger space than normal on his left. He is inviting the forward to shoot and giving himself time to prepare for the save. He is cutting down the choices open to his opponent.

Angles

By changing his position, relative to the goal behind him and the forward in front, a goalkeeper can reduce a forward's target. He can make the normally big goalmouth seem very small indeed.

Try the following test with a team-mate, particularly if you are a goalkeeper. Stand in a good goal scoring position for a forward and put the other player in the correct goal-keeping position *on the goal line*. It could be the position seen in figure 2(a).

Fig. 2(a)

Fig. 2(b)

In figure 2(b) the goalkeeper has taken up a position perhaps halfway towards the player with the ball. Place your friend who is acting as the goalkeeper in this position. How much of the goal can you see? You can appreciate how the second position of the goalkeeper has allowed him to cover more of the goal. He has cut down the target spaces by reducing the shooting angles.

The understanding and judgement of these angles is a most important aspect of goalkeeping skill. Without it you will not go very far in the game.

Positioning for Crosses

Here again the goalkeeper must use a basic position to cover against all eventualities. He is expected to collect all high crosses which come into the goal area. These are his complete responsibility in senior football. Schoolboys and young players may not have the height or spring to do this, but they must always aim to develop the speed, spring and anticipation to allow them to extend and increase their area of command.

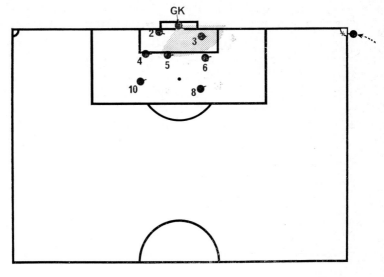

Fig. 3

In figure 3 the goalkeeper has taken up a central position on his goal line and the diagram shows the positions which most defending teams would take up for a corner kick. The goalkeeper will be able to cover the shaded part of the goal area and penalty area easily enough. One of the most difficult corners or crosses to deal with, however, is the one which is aimed to drop on the far corner of the goal area. What can he do about this since to deal with it he must move sideways and backwards?

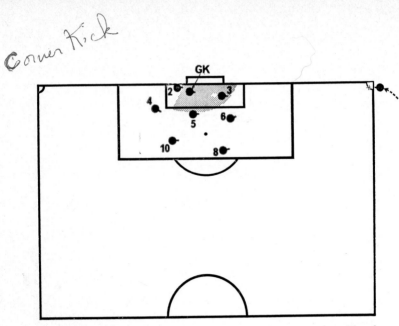

Fig. 4

In figure 4 the goalkeeper is standing by the far upright and a yard or so *off* his goal-line. He is covering much the same area, but is in a much better position relative to the centre of the goal and penalty area. Other defenders are now able to adjust their positions slightly so that the whole of the danger area is more adequately covered. This 'far post' position permits the goalkeeper to see a larger part of the danger area more easily and it allows him the greatest scope for moving forward to meet the ball. Obviously it is easier to move forward quickly than to move backwards.

The important points to remember in making positional judgments involve time and distance. How far away is the person with the ball? How fast can he make the ball travel to reach any given point? A goalkeeper's judgment then means that he has to judge the first two points in relation to his own speed of travel. In figure 4 where the goalkeeper has taken up a position a yard or so off his goal-line he has given himself that amount of 'start' should he have to collect the ball on the edge of, or outside the goal area.

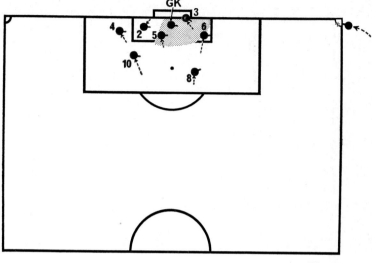

Fig. 5

In high class football an opposing player with a powerful
drive could hit a high fast cross to the near post or upright.
The goalkeeper will be worried by this possibility and he may
adjust his position as in figure 5. Notice how all the other
defenders have re-adjusted their positions accordingly.
The danger area is now increased on the far side of goal,
behind the goalkeeper. No. 4 has moved to cover it, while
No. 3 has gone on to the goal-line since the goalkeeper's
new position means that he need not cover the same part
of the goal area.

Thoughtful attacking play means that attackers must
analyse these positions in the same way as defenders. What
may be a danger point for a defence will be the point at which
attackers try to create advantage. In modern football watch
how attackers move into certain key positions long before
the kick is taken. They try to cancel out the advantages which
a good goalkeeper should have through being able to jump
and use his hands. This is why you may see the following
organisation of attackers.

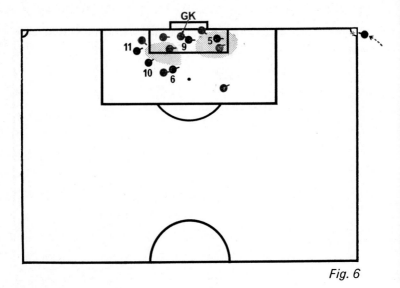

Fig. 6

In figure 6 two tall players, Nos. 9 and 5, have moved right into the goal area. No. 5 is in the dangerous forward part of the goal area to deflect the ball towards goal, or backwards over his head. No. 9 is in the same position as the goalkeeper, with the aim of trying to get to the ball with his head a split second before the goalkeeper. He will also go for goal or attempt a backwards deflection. Attackers 11, 10 and 6 are slightly beyond the area into which the corner kick may go direct, or into which the backwards deflections go.

The attacking team has *two* possibilities of causing trouble in *two* danger areas and the player taking the corner kick has *two* choices of where to aim his kick. In this situation good teams arrange to have the corner kick aimed for certain areas. Other attackers will position themselves to run into these areas as the ball arrives; if they take up positions in these areas beforehand, they attract the attention of defenders before the kick is taken.

Free Kicks

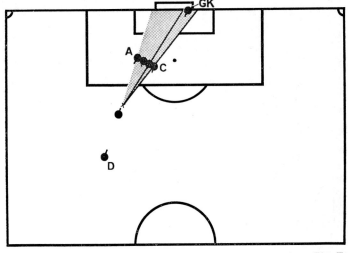

Fig. 7

The basic responsibility for organising a defence when a free kick is to be taken, and the ball is likely to come into the goal area rests with the goalkeeper. He knows what he can cover and he must organise the other defenders to cover danger areas. This must be done quickly, with no discussion or argument. While arguments are going on the ball is likely to be entering the net. These situations must be practised constantly.

In League football, teams probably score 50%–75% of their goals from what are known as 'dead ball' situations—those in which a team has a free play of the ball (corner kicks, free kicks, throw-ins and so on).

In figure 7 a direct free kick has been given about 25 yards from goal. The nearest defender cannot position himself less than 10 yards from the ball and a wall of players, three or four in number, is set up at that distance. The two end players are the most important. You will notice that player **A** has been positioned slightly outside a line between the ball and

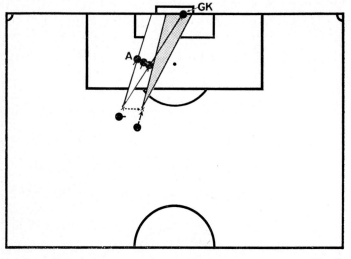

Fig. 8

the post behind him. This is to cover against a shot being swerved around the end of the wall. Player **A** *must* be put in this position by the goalkeeper or, alternatively, by a free player **D** who is behind the ball. Player **A** then stands fast and other players in the wall line up *tightly* together on **A's** left hand side. The goalkeeper must decide whether or not he wants **C** there because with **C** in position the goalkeeper may not have a clear sight of the ball. Without **C** there the ball may be played (as in figure 8) to one side and too much of the goal may be left exposed.

The goalkeeper's decision will be based upon his capabilities for covering a larger area of his goal. He must put himself in a position where he can move forwards, or forwards and sideways, rather than backwards.

Goal Kick Drill

Practice Situations which Test Judgment

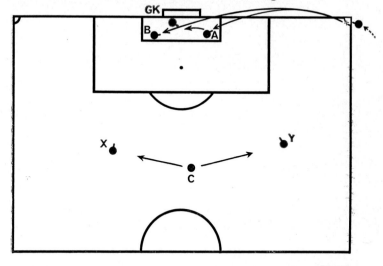

Fig. 9

The Corner Kick (figure 9) is being taken from the right. Two attackers, **A** and **B,** station themselves in the danger positions. Either of two corner kicks can be taken and the goalkeeper must make up his mind very late and quickly. The attackers **A** and **B** operate under a special rule or 'condition'—they must not touch the ball more than three times between them. To add realism the goalkeeper must try to find players **X** and **Y** with a quick throw. He can be challenged and he must remember the 4-step rule. **C** is another opponent who will try to intercept any passes to **X** or **Y**.

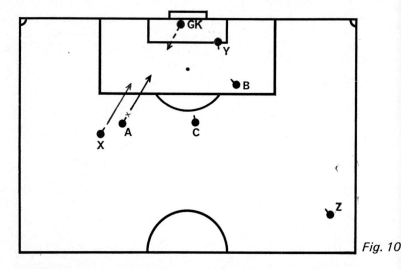

Fig. 10

Narrowing Angles (figure 10) Player **A** sets off at
speed towards the penalty area—defender **X** starts off 5
yards behind him. Attacker **C** can never move inside the
penalty area and attacker **B** is always in the position shown
in the diagram. When he reaches the penalty area attacker **A**
can only shoot or pass to **B**. If he passes to **B**, **B** can only
shoot or pass back to **C**. If the ball is passed to **B**, or if **B**
passes to **C**, the defender **Y** can attempt to prevent a goal
from being scored.

This practice tests the goalkeeper's ability to produce
correct angles.

  (i) He must adopt an angle to reduce the risk of **A** scoring
      with a direct shot.
 (ii) If the ball passes to **B** the goalkeeper must adjust his
      position for the shot from **B**.
(iii) If the ball is played back to **C** a third positional change
      must be made.

The goalkeeper has to change his basic position frequently. When the defence, and particularly the goalkeeper,
gets possession of the ball they must try to hit the target
player **Z** with a long pass as soon as possible.

14

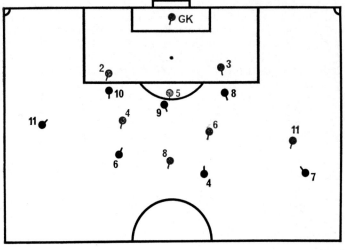

Fig. 11

Free Kicks

In figure 11 an attack is playing against a defence. Seven attackers (the black players) are playing against seven defenders and a goalkeeper, the red team. The attackers will try to work for openings so that the ball can be passed to the feet of black players 8, 9 and 10.

Frequently, but not on every occasion, the goalkeeper or the coach will whistle for a free kick. It may be either direct or indirect. The goalkeeper or coach raises one arm straight above his head if it is an indirect free kick, this being the recognised signal used by referees in these circumstances. This will test the speed of defensive organisation and the goalkeeper's competence in dominating the defensive organisation. This practice is a good one for attackers as well.

The Techniques of Goalkeeping

The goalkeeper, above all else, must be able to stop the ball safely and surely. Therefore, there are certain fundamental principles which are really the rules of goalkeeping. You may not be able to stick to the rules all the time, but if you deliberately ignore them your goalkeeping will be unsafe.

1   Whenever possible a goalkeeper must have as much of his body behind the ball as possible. This applies whether he is jumping, diving, standing or falling to save. Obviously the ball may slip through your hands or between your feet and legs but it cannot slip through your stomach or chest.

2   Just before the ball hits you *relax that part of your body which is being used and draw it away from the direction in which the ball is travelling.* 'Give' with the force of the shot. The same rule really applies to all players. When your inside right catches the ball on his chest he pulls his chest back to prevent the ball from bouncing away. If his chest is sticking out he will lose control of the ball as it bounces away.

3   Never reach for the ball by bending your body sideways or by diving if you can move your feet and get the whole of your body in position. Good goalkeepers make shots look easy, since all the shots seem to be fired straight at them—they have used their feet quickly to get into the right position. Speed of footwork is something without which a goalkeeper is struggling.

4   Catch rather than punch. Punching or palming the ball may be necessary in desperate situations, but if you have a choice, catch the ball. There has never been a great goalkeeper who has not had 'sticky' hands. These are the players whose hands seem to attract the ball like a magnet and once the ball hits them it stays there.

Fielding a Ground Shot

In Photos 1 and 2 notice how the goalkeeper is watching the ball into his hands. No chance here of the ball slipping through any gaps between his legs or between his arms and body—there are none.

In Photo 3 the goalkeeper has taken extra care, perhaps because of dangerous spin on the ball or perhaps the ground is bumpy. The kneeling stance gives maximum cover behind the ball and because he is on one knee he is able to stand up and move away easily. The sideways position is used to avoid the possibility of the knee sticking out towards the ball and causing it to bounce away out of reach.

Photo 1

Photo 2

Photo 3

Photo 4   Photo 5

Photo 6

Some goalkeepers who are good catchers fail to take enough care. Watch the ball all the way into the catching position before moving away to clear it.

Notice how he has shown the same concentration in fielding this chest high drive (Photo 4). The ball is comfortably cradled into his chest and his body has 'given' with the force of the shot. Indeed, so sharp is the goalkeeper's concentration on the ball that he looks as if he has found a puncture in it!

The goalkeeper is showing how to catch a shot at head height in Photo 5. Head and eyes behind the ball, but notice 'the basket' which his hands and fingers have formed (Photo 6), firm spread but not rigid. There will be little danger of the ball escaping.

Photo 7   Photo 8

Catching a High Ball

The position of the hands will provide the basket (Photos 7 and 8). The goalkeeper's problem here is to get the greatest height while holding a balanced position and, at the same time, protecting himself. To jump high, take off on one foot. The stride before you plant your take-off foot is a long one which allows you to swing your free leg, powerfully, forwards and upwards. This 'free leg' swing is most important since it assists you to gain greater height and this is why high jumpers in athletics use it. Secondly, the upward swing of the knee allows your knee and leg to become a 'fender' against the possibility of injury.

You must improve the height of your jump as much as you can and, even more important, your ability to catch the ball safely as high as you can. If you wait for it to drop to an easy height, tall attackers will head it almost out of your hands and into the net. Avoid, if you can, situations in which you have to jump from a standing position and particularly those in which all your jump is vertically upwards. If your jump is forwards (towards the ball) and upwards you will gain greater height. Other players will tend to get out of your way and you will be less liable to make catching errors, especially those which may be caused by jostling from opponents.

Photo 9

Turning the Ball over the Bar and Punching Clear

Catch the ball whenever you can! Occasionally, however, a catch is dangerous and it is safer to turn the ball for a corner kick or to punch clear. The accent must be on the safety of your goal.

Here (Photo 9) the goalkeeper has the time in which to take extra care in putting the ball over the bar and he has used two hands to do so. More often, when under pressure from attackers near to his goal-line, the goalkeeper will use one hand. A general rule is that the hand which is furthest away from goal will be used. This allows a full swing of the hand and arm to push the ball in the direction in which you want it to go. Reaching as high as possible with one hand is easier than with two. Try it against a wall.

A golden rule for goalkeepers in this situation, where you are giving away a corner kick, is to make certain by knocking it well over the bar and behind the goal. Some goalkeepers try to flick the ball away. This looks spectacular and exciting. But it involves greater risk and risky goalkeepers lose matches.

The situation in which most goalkeepers have to consider punching is when a high pass, played into the penalty area, is being chased by forwards and defenders who are watching the ball (Photo 10). They are on a collision course and since they are not able to judge their challenge with the goalkeeper's movement, collision will make catching less safe, with the additional possibility of injury to the goalkeeper. The goalkeeper must be decisive—hesitation will be fatal.

1 Make your run early and confidently.
2 Concentrate on the flight of the ball all the time. Forget that other players are on the field.
3 Punch with two fists rather than one.
4 Punch through the ball not at it.

You should aim to clear the player who passed the ball in your direction. As far as possible and as hard as possible— that should be the goalkeeper's aim. No half measures.

Occasionally goalkeepers have to punch crosses away from goal. Use the hand and arm which is nearest to goal, or if you

Photo 10

like, the hand and arm which is furthest from the direction in which the ball will be punched. As with turning the ball over the bar, your natural arm swing is then in the right direction.

Don't pat the ball: hit it. Most goalkeepers say that the high cross which is aimed to land beyond them in the goal area causes most difficulty. Try not to flick at the ball as you are jumping backwards. Leave it late, turn and run after the ball so that you can then jump and knock the ball well clear of the penalty area. When you go for the difficult ball remember that all players are a nuisance, even your own team-mates. They can impede you just as much as opposing players. Be prepared to move them by your determined run and jump, and always be aggressive. Polite goalkeepers may be nice to know, but they don't win matches!

Diving to Save

Photo 11

This shot of a goalkeeper in action is probably the most common example of photographs of goalkeepers (Photo 11). The diving save, where the goalkeeper is in mid-air and travelling at top speed, is one of the most thrilling sights in football. It is usually produced as a speedy reaction to a snap shot.

Even here, however, there are points which a young goalkeeper must think about and practise. Notice how the goalkeeper's face is always in 'the window'. This is not to suit the photographer but to produce the best position, in fact the only position, in which the goalkeeper can watch the ball into his hands. The sideways position is very important when diving. Similarly, if the shot comes towards his chest or stomach the goalkeeper is putting the largest area of his body behind the ball. Safety first again!

Diving and catching in this spectacular way is often necessary but it is no use doing it well and catching the ball safely if, on landing, you drop the ball or allow it to roll out of your grasp. As soon as you have caught the ball draw it into your chest or stomach, and begin to draw your knees up as well, even while you are still in mid-air. As you hit the ground there will be less likelihood of the shock of your landing dislodging the ball.

Ground shots often cause goalkeepers great problems. Diving upwards or horizontally sideways is one thing, but diving downwards is a difficult skill. The sideways principle still holds good. If you dive chest downwards on to the ball it may slip underneath you. If you dive sideways behind the ball you are more likely to stop it. Most dives or jumps are the result of an overbalance in the direction in which you want to go, followed by, almost instantaneously, a powerful thrust from your legs. The more you want to dive sideways the more important the leg furthest away from your intended direction becomes. If you are diving to your left your right leg gives you the push and vice-versa.

What about diving downwards? Many goalkeepers say that you should collapse rather than dive. Just drop in fact. Try it with another goalkeeper. One of you should try to dive on to a ball as fast as possible while, on the same signal, the other drops or collapses on to the ball. Who touched the ball first? In any case, pull the ball into your stomach as soon as you have collected it.

Photo 12   Photo 13

Photo 14

Diving at an Opponent's Feet

We have seen how a goalkeeper can present an opposing
forward with a small target, if he is willing to come forward
as the forward prepares to shoot. The goalkeeper narrows
the forward's shooting angle. Occasionally, if he is quick
enough, the goalkeeper may be able to dive at the opponent's
feet and block the shot. This requires courage, confidence
and great skill.

In Photo 12 the goalkeeper has dived forwards and sideways towards the ball as the forward prepares to shoot with his right foot. Notice how the ball will be collected between the arms and hands rather than the hands alone. Equally important, if the forward goes through with his kick the goalkeeper can use his left arm to absorb some of the force of the kick by using it as 'a fender' towards the attacker's right shin. This will not hurt the attacker and may prevent serious injury to the goalkeeper.

In Photo 13 we can see how quickly the goalkeeper has cradled the ball into his chest. Photo 14 shows this safe position even more clearly. Once again the sideways diving and covering position has given added safety. When diving in this fashion, try to use your body to build a wall between the goal and the ball.

Tricks and feints are a recognised part of a footballer's skill and the goalkeeper can also use them in his highly specialised position. When diving to save, or at an opponent's feet, a goalkeeper can use a feint to gain advantage. If you sway in one direction you may cause the attacker to shoot or to move in the opposite direction. Since you expect this to happen you are ready for it. If you rush out from goal towards an oncoming attacker he will beat you easily. If you move out quickly and then slow down you may find that the attacker slows down as well. Any movement which you make will tend to confuse your opponent and since he will be aiming for a target, the goal, you are making the target difficult to judge. Never allow an opponent a free shot. Try to put him off as much as you can.

One famous goalkeeper when faced with an opponent who had been presented with a clear run and shot at goal would put on a completely 'couldn't care less' attitude, giving the impression that a goal was a certainty and that he would not try to stop it. On many occasions this caused the attacker to take the shot casually when he would be surprised to find the goalkeeper suddenly alert and prepared to save. Remember this when you are facing a skilful attacker: 'Eyes can tell lies'. If you watch his eyes he will fool you. His feet can never lie and, after all, they are the things he will kick the ball with. Great goalkeepers become **very** skilful at 'reading' feet.

Clearing or Using the Ball

Photo 15

Photo 16

The goalkeeper has a responsibility for setting up attacking movements as soon as he has possession of the ball. The law which restricts a goalkeeper's movements when he has gained possession of the ball is very important in modern football. *Remember you cannot take more than four steps when you are holding the ball, bouncing the ball or throwing it in the air unless you release it so that it is played by another player.* If you do, an indirect free kick will be given to your opponents and it will be in a very dangerous part of the field. In these circumstances a goalkeeper can do one of two things. He can use the ball quickly within four paces from the point at which he collected it, or he can drop the ball and dribble it to that part of the penalty area from which he intends to kick or throw the ball. If you do the latter, remember that you can be challenged for the ball in the same way as any other player when you are out of the goal-area.

The accurate long kick deep into your opponents' half of the field is very useful when clearing your defence and as a surprise attacking weapon. The throw, particularly when it is delivered very quickly over 20–30 yards is perhaps more often used, since it ensures that your team keeps possession of the ball and it is accurate. For a long throw a goalkeeper uses the long over-arm slinging technique, but for the shorter distance a basketball or javelin throwing technique is used.

In Photos 15 and 16 the ball is supported by the palm of the hand which is behind it. The arm is pulled quickly back and, with elbow leading, thrown quickly forward. The feet are fairly wide apart and the body is in a 'side on' position in relation to the direction of throw. As the arm begins to move forward, the trunk is turned quickly from side-on to face-on and the arm whips through into the throw. This type of throw is powerful and allows for great accuracy particularly when you wish to deliver the ball quickly to another player's feet. The goalkeeper throws the ball in much the same way as you would throw a cricket ball.

Kicking

There are great advantages to be gained by developing this skill. The greater distance available to the goalkeeper who can kick well out of his hands means that surprise attacking movements can be set up very quickly. Too many goalkeepers, even in top class football, merely try to kick as far as they can without thinking about the easiest and most accurate method of gaining distance. There are certain principles involved in long kicking whether we are considering a goalkeeper or a full back. If you don't understand these principles you will not develop a long kick however hard you try to hit the ball. When you make contact with the ball:

(i)   Your foot must be travelling *as fast as possible*.

(ii) Your leg and foot must be *as long as possible*.

(iii) Your body (your weight) must continue to move forward in the direction of your kick. This means that you must kick *through the ball rather than at it*.

What does this mean to the goalkeeper who is kicking out of his hands?

(a) The ball is *held in one hand*, at *full arm stretch*, in front of your kicking foot and *down towards it*.

(b) The non-kicking leg is also stretched to its fullest extent.

(c) Because of (b) you will now be able to swing your kicking leg in a stretched position as you hit the ball.

(d) As you hit the ball you are almost upright and easily balanced. Immediately after kicking the ball you will overbalance slightly in the direction of your kick.

If you are in doubt remember in which direction you tend to fall immediately after kicking. If your body twists to one side or tends to topple backwards, your kicking force has only partly gone in the direction required. A good kick is really a long, powerful, lifting movement with your leg and foot. Against a strong wind you may find the half volley kick to be more effective. It is less powerful but it keeps the ball much lower and the wind cannot get hold of it so easily.

If you are a good kicker when you have the ball in your hands don't show your skill and power too soon in a game. Give a few easy kicks early in the game and then, when the opposing defence is well forward and perhaps square, you can loft your big kick high into the space behind them.

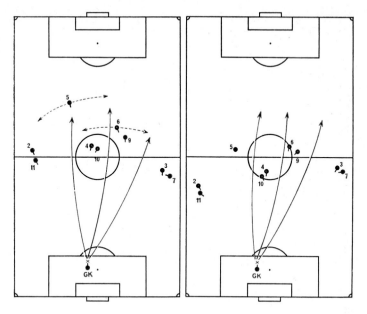

Fig. 12   *Fig. 13*

Figure 12 shows a defence which will intercept your most powerful kick easily. Figure 13 is the position of a defence when it is wide open to the big one out of your hands.

Setting up Attacking Moves from a Goalkeeper's Throw

For all players on the field there are what are known as 'easy choice passes', and effective or penetrating passes. Easy passes are those where there is no risk of your pass being intercepted, usually because it does not threaten danger to the opposing team. Penetration passes are those which travel to a team mate who is well within or behind an opposing defence.

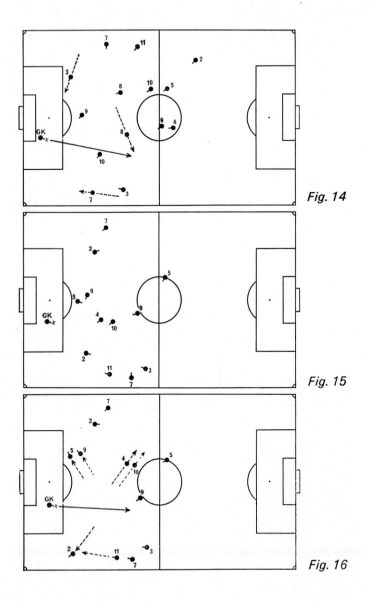

Fig. 14

Fig. 15

Fig. 16

30

In figure 14 the goalkeeper can throw easily to his own No. 7 or No. 3. The opposing team will not be worried since these throws are not dangerous. A better choice would be to aim for the space into which No. 8 is running, since the throw will arrive into space behind the black forwards 7, 8, 9 and 10 and even behind the left back (black No. 3). Almost half of the opposing team has been beaten by this throw. Other players should move to help the goalkeeper by clearing space for penetration passes in exactly the same way as they must move to clear space for other players. This is known as 'moving off the ball' and is a very important football skill.

In figure 15 the goalkeeper's chance of throwing or kicking a good pass to red No. 9, who is unmarked, has been spoiled by his own team-mates hanging about in front of him, particularly red defenders 2, 4 and 5.

In figure 16 red No. 2 has run wide and red No. 5 has done the same in the opposite direction. They could call for the ball and attract the attention of opponents. Red No. 4 is running across field and forward; his nearest opponent dare not let him continue unmarked. The space has been cleared by these 'off the ball runs' for the goalkeeper's throw to the unmarked red No. 9. These tactical plans are simple and can be arranged easily through a little practice and discussion between the goalkeeper and his team-mates.

Skill Practice
1 Punching Clear
In figure 17 a channel has been marked out parallel with the edge of the penalty area and 15 yards from it. Three opponents start in this channel. Player **X** kicks or throws a high pass to land in the penalty area. As soon as the pass is commenced, one or two players from **A**, **B** and **C** can attempt to score. Begin with one only. The goalkeeper must punch so that the ball clears the remaining two players in the channel towards the server **X**. If it doesn't, the opponents can try to score with a first-time shot or perhaps a lob. To begin with **X** should throw or kick the high pass near the goalkeeper on his goal line. This will give him confidence. As this becomes easy the high pass should be delivered nearer to the edge of the penalty area so that he has to run out quickly and judge his jump and punch carefully.

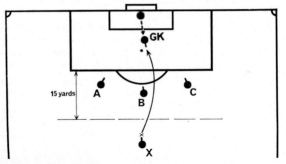

Fig. 17

2 Fielding the Ball

The goalkeeper must experience the conditions in which he will have to field the ball in a game and he will need the help of other players to obtain realistic practice. In figure 18 the goalkeeper takes up position on his goal line and two servers, **X** and **Y**, each with a ball, stand on or just outside the penalty area. **X** and **Y** drive straight firm kicks at the goalkeeper who moves to field them. These kicks can represent firm back passes or long range shots. As soon as the ball is

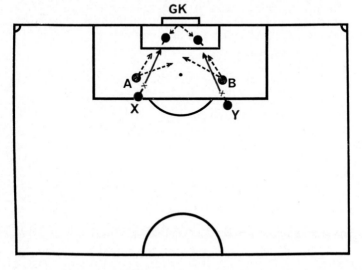

Fig.

kicked by **X** or **Y**, **A** and **B**, who represent attackers, can move towards the goalkeeper. If he fails to field the ball cleanly they will pounce on the loose ball and try to score. Perhaps once in every five or six kicks, **X** or **Y** will drive the ball towards the goal but rather wide of the goalkeeper.

These surprise shots will keep him mentally alert. Practice must never become routine and mechanical. The goalkeeper above all players must be ready for the unexpected.

In figure 19 seven players stand in the penalty area in front of the goalkeeper. Servers **X**, **Y** and **Z** drive low shots towards the goalkeeper through the players in the penalty area. **X**, **Y** and **Z** will change position to do so. The goalkeeper is now getting practice in the situation when, in the game, his vision may be obstructed in this way.

Most times the players in the penalty area must not interfere with the ball, stepping aside or letting it pass through their legs at the last moment. Occasionally, however, one may flick at the ball just as it passes him. This will keep the goalkeeper from going through mechanical practice. As the ball passes them, the back four players in the penalty area can turn and score from any drives which the goalkeeper fails to field cleanly.

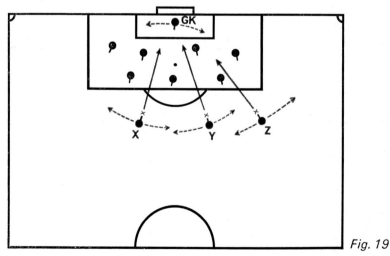

Fig. 19

3 Saving from a Rebound Wall or Shooting Board

A Rebound Wall or a Shooting Board used with a sand pit
or on a grass pitch can provide valuable practice for a
goalkeeper. Landing mattresses in a gymnasium and a plain
gymnasium wall can serve the same purpose.

In figure 20 the goalkeeper, **Z**, stands facing the wall while
servers, **X** and **Y**, are behind and to one side of him. **Z** must
face the wall all the time. Taking it in turn **X** and **Y** kick or
throw the ball against the wall and **Z** must save the rebound. In this way **Z** cannot see the ball until very late and
he has to 'read' the angle and pace of the rebound very
quickly. To make the practice increasingly difficult **Z** takes
up a position nearer to the wall. Servers **X** and **Y** can vary
the angle at which the ball rebounds to the goalkeeper by
changing the angle of their kick or throw on to the wall.

If a particularly bumpy rebound surface or wall is available,
the goalkeeper can obtain a great deal of useful practice for
himself without assistance. Training alone is never enjoyable
and rarely effective.

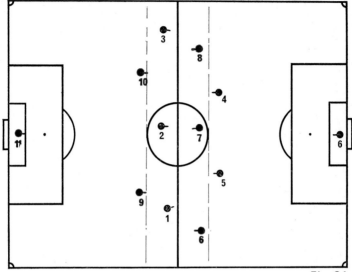

Fig. 21

4 Target Kicking

Kicking the ball out of his hands and using the whole of his penalty area (remember the 4-step law), red goalkeeper No. 11 tries to find one of the three attackers on his side, Nos. 6, 7 and 8 in their zone (figure 21). If he is successful these players will turn and attack the goal at the opposite end of the field, which is guarded by No. 6 and defended by black players 4 and 5. When the attack has been completed, whether successfully or unsuccessfully, the players will return to their positions and goalkeeper No. 6 will try the same thing, aiming for his own attackers, black 1, 2 and 3. If successful they will turn and attack towards the red goal against Nos. 9 and 10.

If the goalkeeper's kick lands in the wrong zone, e.g. if red No. 11's kick lands in the black zone occupied by 1, 2 and 3, they will set up an attack towards the red goal—just as they would in the game. At no time can the different groups of players move into another group of players' zone *unless* they have possession of the ball.

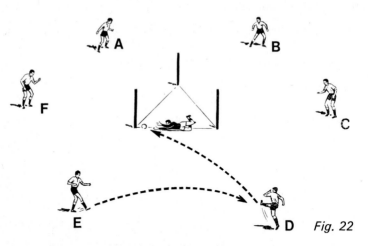

Fig. 22

5 Reaction and Judgment Practice

(a) In figure 22 three improvised goals are made by placing three posts in the form of a triangle. The width of the goals should be rather less than the eight yards of a normal goal. Six players, **A, B, C, D, E** and **F,** position themselves 15–20 yards away from the goals in a circle. The ball is passed between them and frequent sharp shots are taken. The goalkeeper changes his position within the three goals as the position of the ball changes.

This practice gives a goalkeeper experience in judging his position relative to the goal. This he must do in the game. It is also good agility practice and provides enjoyable shooting practice for a fairly large group of attackers.

(b) In figure 23 **A** and **B** attack down the wing to hit a cross into the goal area. In this area **C** and **D** are attackers who try to score and the goalkeeper in dealing with the attack is assisted by one defender **Y**. As the attack is completed the ball is played up field to **E** and **F**, who attack the opposite flank. **Y** moves out to oppose them and defender **X** takes up his position in the goal-mouth assisting his goalkeeper. The three attacking pairs can rotate their positions at the same time so that

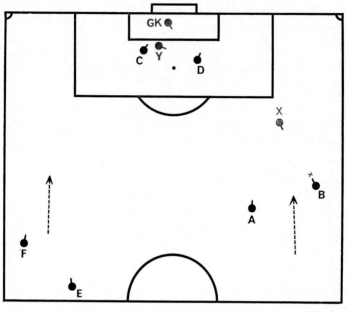

Fig. 23

they take turns in attacking down each side of the field and in the centre.

The goalkeeper has to judge realistic crosses and his position relative to the attackers and his defender in the goalmouth.

Personal Training

A goalkeeper must be supple, strong and quick. Strength must be of the power variety since he has to 'lift' or 'throw' his body as far as he can, as fast as he can to make saves or interceptions. All these things are important and a goalkeeper should devote at least 30 minutes of his practice and training time to a personal fitness programme and this programme should be a daily routine. Yes, every day!

Jumping and Springing Activities

1 Jump Rolls (fig. 24)

From a standing position do a forward roll and immediately follow the roll with a very high jump. Repeat five times without stopping. Rest for 30 seconds and repeat. Each series of jumps with the following rest is one stint. Start by doing three stints and work up to ten over two or three weeks.

Different rolls—forwards, sideways and backwards—may be used.

Do the rolls and jumps holding a ball in two hands all the time.

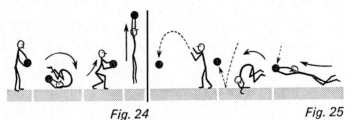

Fig. 24   Fig. 25

2 Roll and Catch (fig. 25)

Throw the ball fairly high in the air about 3–4 feet to one side of your standing position. Perform a quick roll (backwards, forwards or sideways). As soon as your feet touch the ground after completing the roll, dive or jump to catch the bouncing ball.

Set yourself targets:
  (a) Catch the ball before it bounces three times.
  (b) Catch the ball before it bounces twice.
  (c) As you progress don't throw the ball so high.

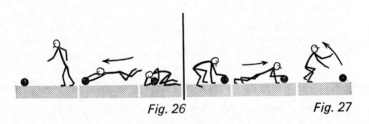

Fig. 26   Fig. 27

3 Dive, Catch and Roll *(fig. 26)*

Place the ball 10 feet away from your standing position. Dive to catch the ball and, as in the game, pull the ball into your stomach and complete a roll. Increase the distance a few inches each time.

With a little imagination many interesting and challenging jumping activities can be devised, all of which can improve your jumping and diving ability if you extend your personal targets. Group a number of repetitions together and call this number one training stint. With a short rest in between, set yourself a number of training stints. Increase your training as it becomes easy for you.

Strength and Suppleness *(fig. 27)*

In the crouch position place one hand on the ground and one hand on the ball. Keeping your feet still, perhaps behind a mark on the ground, walk forward as far as you can, using one hand on the ground and the other on the ball. Find the furthest position at which you can leave the ball and push yourself back into position behind the starting mark. The ball must remain where it is and your free hand can only be used as a push off. Try the same activity with two hands on the ball.

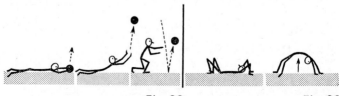

Fig. 28   Fig. 29

Take up a position lying full length face downwards on the ground with the ball held at arms' length beyond your head (figure 28). From this position throw the ball as high as you can using your stretched arms only. Get to your feet and catch the ball before it bounces a second time.

Great goalkeepers must be supple and strong in the back and shoulders. Supple because a stiff goalkeeper cannot get into the many different body positions required of a goalkeeper in making diving saves. Strong because these positions have to be assumed in a split second and often when opponents are making a challenge.

Back Bridge *(fig. 29)*
Lying on your back place your hands beneath your shoulders and, with your feet flat on the ground, press your body into a full arch clear of the ground. Once again set yourself a number of stints.

When you have pressed up into the back bridge take alternate hands off the ground and then alternate legs. Then try to support yourself in the bridge position on one hand and one foot only.

Rockers *(fig. 30)*
Lying full length face downwards, clasp your hands behind your neck and stretch your body as much as you can. Beginning gradually, rock your body from head to knees, as high as you can.

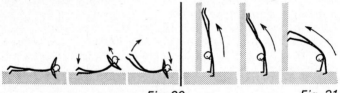

Fig. 30   Fig. 31

Bridge Hand Stands *(fig. 31)*
Placing your hands about 2 feet away from the wall kick up into a hand stand. Repeat the hand stand, moving your hands a little further away from the wall each time.

Football is a great game because it is designed to allow each individual player to give as much as he can within simple rules. Success demands unselfishness and team work at a very high level indeed. The goalkeeper is a very important member of a football team and he needs assistance to make his practice and training sessions worth the time and trouble. Give him this help and the valuable practice which he gets through your assistance will pay great dividends in team play. Practice does not necessarily make you perfect, but it qoes a long way towards helping.

BACK DEFENDERS

CONTENTS

A few years ago a manager looking for full backs or centre half backs would require, first of all, a report on the size of likely candidates. If you were not big enough it was assumed that you would not be good enough to fill these positions in the team. This was in the days when backs and half backs defended and forwards attacked. The wingers and the centre forward were not required to accept any defensive responsibilities and, similarly, the full backs and the centre half had little responsibility for attacking play. Before the introduction of the present offside law in 1925 things were different. A player was offside if he was *nearer to the opponents' goal line than the ball* at the moment the ball was played UNLESS *three* of his opponents were nearer to their own goal line than himself. The present offside law only requires two of his opponents to be nearer to their own goal line in these circumstances. The old law produced too great an advantage for defensive players. They were able to mark tightly near to the half way line and have almost unbeatable cover at the same time.

In figure 1 we can see the system of defensive positioning which MIGHT HAVE BEEN used at that time. One full back (No. 2) very near to the half way line and the other full back (No. 3) covering him.

Opposing wingers marked by the half backs (Nos. 4 and 6) with the centre half back (No. 5) being allowed to operate as a free central attacking or supporting player.

If attackers attempt to move into the red team's defending half of the field, No. 2 may step forward and leave them offside. Even if he makes a mistake in timing his movement forward, his mistake can be covered by the covering back (No. 3), and the goalkeeper.

With the change in the offside law a good deal of the safety involved in a team's use of offside tactics was removed.

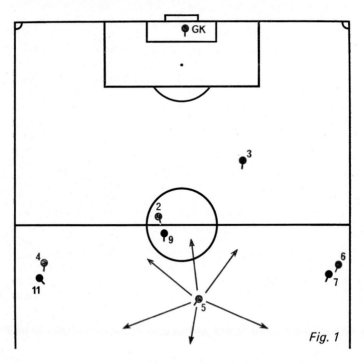

Fig. 1

In figure 2 the forward players have much more freedom to move into their opponents' half of the field. So long as two red opponents are nearer to their own goal-line than the ball at the moment it is played, they cannot be off-side.

What was the result? The birth of modern systems of play and tactical developments.

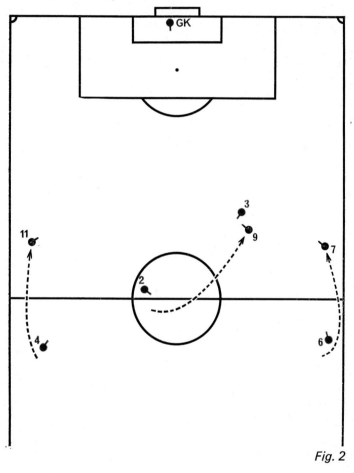

Fig. 2

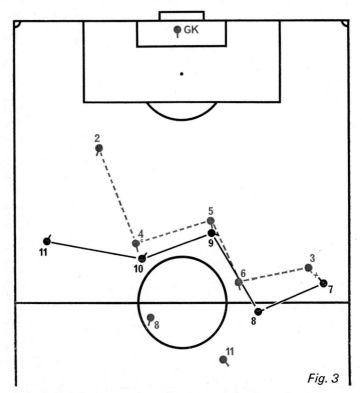

Fig. 3

In figure 3 we can see the re-organisation of a team to counter the change in the offside law. Three backs (Nos. 2, 5 and 3) are used to form the last defensive unit of players. Where No. 3, the left back, is challenging for the ball with the opposing No. 7, No. 5 remains the central back but in a position to move across behind No. 3. Behind No. 5, the right back, No. 2, can swing across to cover the central area *if* No. 5 has to move over. This is the 3 Back Pivot system. It is named the Pivot system because with the centre half, No. 5, the central point, both the full backs, Nos. 2 and 3, swing in front of No. 5 or behind him according to whether they are marking or covering. What do we mean when we say a

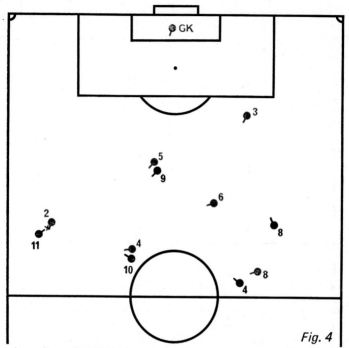

Fig. 4

player is marked? If you are marking an opponent closely you
must be in a position:

   (a) Between that opponent and YOUR OWN goal;
   (b) To see the opponent and the ball at the same time
       WITHOUT having to turn to do so;
   (c) Near enough to the opponent so that if the ball is
       passed to him you can intercept it or tackle for it at the
       same time as he tries to control or play it.

   In figure 4 where the red team is defending and the opposing No. 11 has the ball, most of the attacking team are well
marked, but one player is badly marked. Which is the
unmarked player? Check the three marking rules. That's
right, the attacking No. 8 is in a position in which the nearest
defender, No. 6, cannot watch him and the ball safely and
easily.

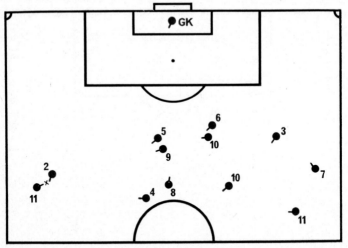

Fig. 5

In figure 5 a similar situation has occurred. Which attacking player, where the red team is defending and the attacking No. 11 has the ball, is badly marked?

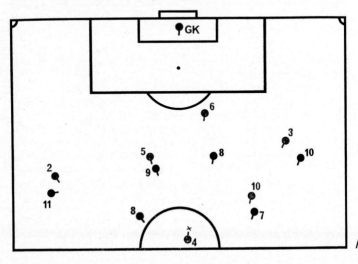

Fig. 6

In figure 6 a serious problem for the defending team has occurred. Attacking player No. 4 has broken clear with the ball. Red No. 8 will probably move to challenge but one other attacker is unmarked. Which player is it? You are right, attacking player No. 8 has been allowed to move clear of his nearest opponent No. 6. Is No. 6 playing well or badly if he allows this to happen?

In this position No. 6 is right because he has to cover the player nearest to him who is his own No. 5. If No. 6 followed his opponent (No. 8) closely he would leave the defence 'square' with a possibility of a through pass from No. 4 causing the chance of a shot at goal. The decision when to mark tight and when to cover is the MOST IMPORTANT judgment which a defender has to make. If he is a back player he will have to make the decision often and very quickly. Back defenders must never allow space to be made behind them into which the ball can be played and into which an attacker can run.

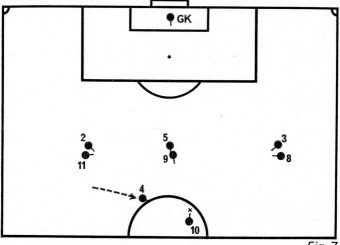

Fig. 7

In figure 7 three defending players, the back players Nos. 2, 5 and 3, are marking opponents tightly but there is no cover. The opposing No. 10 is free with the ball although the

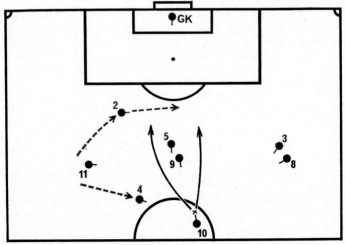

Fig. 8

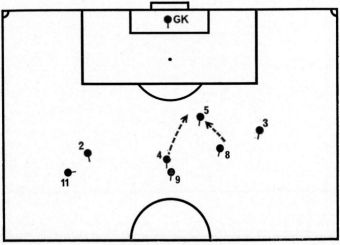

Fig. 9

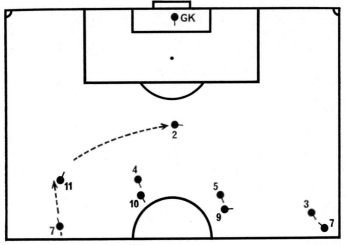

Fig. 10

defending No. 4 is recovering to make a challenge. Which of the three back players should cover his team-mates rather than mark tightly? That's right, No. 2 MUST cover. The most difficult pass which No. 10 can try is to his team-mate No. 11 because he has to pass across the defending No. 4. We can see the covering position in figure 8. No. 2 can now move to cover any pass which is aimed to drop in the space behind Nos. 5 and 3. This is good defensive play. Let us examine some of the back systems used in modern football.

In figure 9 we see a unit of four back players in which Nos. 4 and 5 pivot to cover the centre of the field. In the diagram there is a possibility of the ball being played to the opposing centre forward, No. 9. The red No. 5 leaves his opponent to cover behind No. 4. If the pass looks likely to go to No. 8, red No. 5 will mark him closely while No. 4, this time, leaves his man and moves to cover behind No. 5.

In figure 10 we can see what is often known as the Bolt system, so called because the movement of the covering player (No. 2 in this case) resembles the action of a sliding door bolt. If play is moving towards the left side of the defence, the full back on the other side moves into a full central covering position behind the other defenders. This has happened in the diagram. If play threatens the right side of the defence, No. 2 *marks* tight while No. 3 moves into the full central covering position. No. 3 then becomes the 'bolt'. In some teams the defending team's winger (No. 7) drops back to cut out the possibility of a pass being given to the unmarked player.

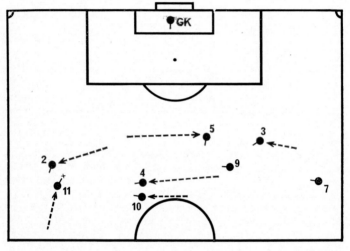

Fig. 11

In figure 11, instead of sharing the central cover, red defenders No. 5 and No. 4 have decided that No. 4 will always move to mark and challenge any player who looks like receiving the ball. No. 5 always slides across to cover behind him and the 'far side' full back (the full back farthest away from the ball) slides into a half-covering position. In the diagram, No. 3 is moving into this position. In doing so he calculates that, even if the attacking side can send a pass to the player he should be marking, the pass will not be dangerous.

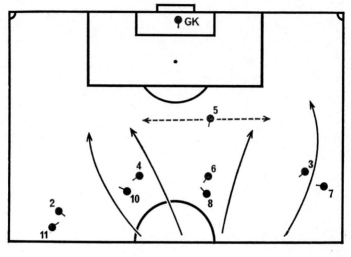

Fig. 12

'Sweepers'

The next stage which has developed has caused one player to be placed permanently behind all the other defenders who are marking opponents tightly. This free defender or 'sweeper' is not responsible for marking any one opponent, but he is totally responsible for all cover across the full width of the field.

In figure 12 we can see the sweeper (No. 5) in position. The clever player in this position will often leave a space into which he tempts the opposing team to play 'through' passes. In doing so he knows that he can intercept these passes before an opposing forward can reach them.

What happens when the sweeper is drawn out of position? The basic rule of covering must apply. *That defender who is farthest from the ball must cover.*

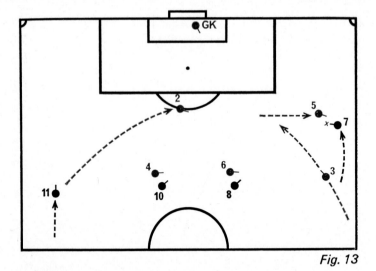

Fig. 13

In figure 13 where the sweeper, No. 5, has had to move out to the wing to check a breakthrough by the opposing No. 7, the far side full back, No. 2, has accepted the final covering responsibility. The beaten full back (No. 3) will recover as fast as he can into the central position which has been left by 'the sweeper' and, when he gets back into position, No. 2 will return to his marking responsibility against the opposing No. 11.

Fundamentals of Back Play

The first requirement of a back is to defend. That is to say, *he must prevent opponents from running past him, with or without the ball.* To be effective he must know when to 'jockey' an opponent, or guide him into a 'safe' part of the field. The back must know when to try to intercept a pass and when to tackle. Finally, and of great importance, he must never become 'a ball watcher'. THESE are the players to whom the movement of the ball acts like a magnet. They watch the ball and fail to watch the dangerous and cunning positioning of attackers near to goal. Let us examine these aspects of back play more closely.

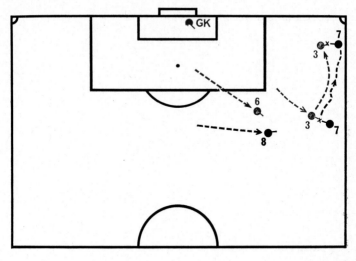

Fig. 14

1. Jockeying

In figure 14 the ball has been played to the attacking No. 7 out on the wing. Player No. 8 is moving quickly to support and unless the defending back (No. 3) is careful a situation will arise in which two attackers (Nos. 8 and 7) are playing against one defender (No. 3).

No. 3, realising the danger, approaches his opponent so that he leaves an inviting space down the wing. He forces No. 7 to hold the ball and move down the wing. As this happens the back shadows his movement but does not attempt to tackle until he has 'jockeyed' No. 7 deep in the corner of the field.

2. Intercepting

It is always better to intercept the ball than to tackle for it. Backs must be careful, however, because being the last defenders (other than the goalkeeper), opponents will try to deceive them into coming out from goal and taking risks.

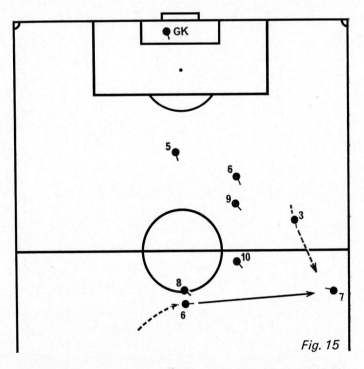

Fig. 15

In figure 15, the full back, No. 3, has spotted the possibility of a pass from the opposing No. 6 to No. 7. He has gone for an interception and he is in a safe position to do so. Why?

(a) The attempt to intercept is being made in the opponents' half of the field. This means that if No. 3 makes a mistake he has a chance to recover.

(b) He has elected to try the interception because he knows that there are other defenders (Nos. 5, 6 and 10) near enough to cover him if he fails.

(c) The risk of making a mistake is worth taking since, if he is successful he will find himself in possession of the ball and moving close to the opposing team's penalty area.

Look at figure 16. A pass is about to be played from the attacking No. 10 to No. 7. What should the defending No. 3 do? Intercept, tackle or hold a position close to No. 7? That's right, if he tries to intercept or tackle, No. 7 could play the ball back to No. 8 or perhaps let the ball go to No. 2. No risks in this part of the field!

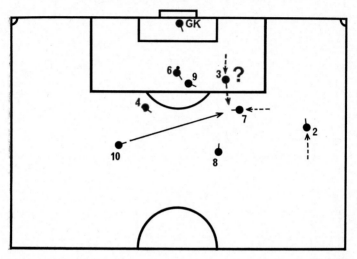

Fig. 16

3. Tackling

Full backs must never take risks except when they are well away from goal and when they are well covered. Defending well means tackling well and there are certain important points to remember when approaching a tackle.

(a) Judge your tackle so that you play the ball just as your opponent attempts to play it.

(b) Concentrate entirely on the ball; opponents will try all kinds of movements or feints to fool you. Once you have decided to tackle it is the ball that matters.

(c) Your angle of approach should be such as to make it impossible for your opponent to move in the direction which suits him IF you miss your tackle.

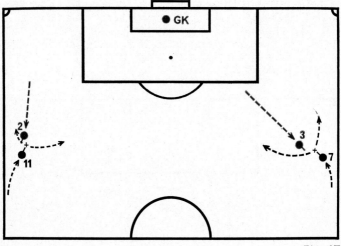

Fig. 17

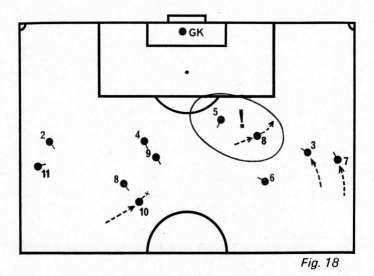

Fig. 18

In figure 17 the angle used by full back No. 3 to approach and tackle the opposing No. 7, who has the ball, allows No. 7 a fairly free choice of direction to avoid the tackle. On the opposite side of the field, full back No. 2 has used a much steeper approach angle. The opposing No. 11 will have difficulty in moving down the touch line. If he evades the tackle he will have to move 'in field'—probably on to his weaker foot.

That's a good point for all defenders to remember. Learn as much about your opponent as soon as you can in the match. Is he able to use one foot much better than the other? If this is so you will be able to anticipate his likely choice of direction whenever he has the ball. Try to force your opponent to use his weaker foot.

4. Ball Watching

In figure 18 where No. 10 has the ball the defending No. 5 is far more interested in watching the ball than watching the movement of the opposing No. 8 into a dangerous position. Remember the rules about marking and covering. Ball watchers are irresponsible and bad players because they do not appreciate their duties towards other defenders. Good defence is a matter of a group of players depending upon each other. The defender who plays on his own and for himself is a poor footballer.

5. Collective Defence

A team which has sound defensive organisation possesses back players who fully understand the requirements of collective defence. What are these requirements and even more important, what are they defending?

   (i) Back players, in common with all players who are defending at any moment in the game, must realise that their responsibility is to defend their goal. This sounds obvious but watch your next match closely and you will see defenders trying to defend in parts of the field where safe defence is impossible.

Fig. 19

in figure 19 we can see the CONCENTRATION of a defence in and around the danger area (shaded). Attackers who move into the danger area must be marked tightly. The farther away from this area they are, the less dangerous they are.

(ii) From all parts of the field defenders will fall back in the face of an attack to guard the danger area. If they are in doubts about the safety of their goal they will RETREAT and FUNNEL back towards goal.

In figure 20 we can see a side disposed as it might be at the moment at which an attack breaks down and its opponents gain possession of the ball. This is the time at which the team shown is open to a quick counter attack. Look at the space behind the back defenders and look at the space between them.

In figure 21 we see the same team organised to set up the first stage of firm defence near to the half way line. All players have fallen back towards their own goal, they have moved from wide loose positions to narrow and tighter positions. At this stage Nos. 7, 8 and 10 may begin to force opponents to play across the field in front of the defensive organisation.

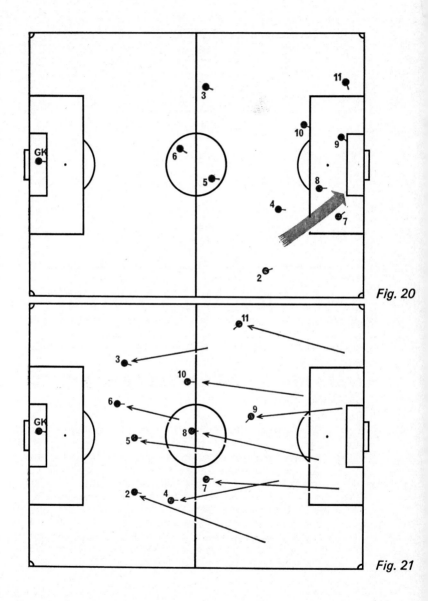

Fig. 20

Fig. 21

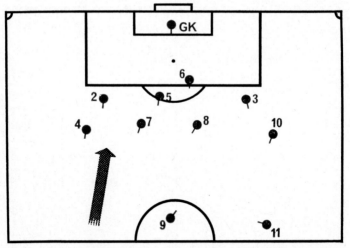

Fig. 2

They will try for interceptions and tackles *when they are very sure* of success. If the opposing attack continues to move forward we can see the final concentration in figure 22. The spaces between defenders are very narrow and the whole defence is tight and compact. At this stage determined efforts will be made to prevent any further attacking movements towards goal.

TECHNIQUES WHICH MUST BE MASTERED BY THE BACK

Tackling

A good back player must master the different techniques of tackling. To be a good tackler he must:

  (a) Concentrate on the ball and refuse to be tempted into making a movement because of an opponent's trickery until he is sure that he can strike at the ball.

  (b) Be quick into and out of the tackle. The back who 'dives' into a tackle with all his effort and weight may be successful some of the time but when he is beaten his opponent will have a clear and unchallenged run towards goal. Balance is important since it allows you to change direction and position quickly.

(c) Have determination never to give up. If an opponent tricks you two or three times you must adjust your position or try something different. If he beats you by going down the wing, try to make him move across the field. If he beats you by dodging and feinting make him change his mind by dodging and feinting yourself as you prepare to tackle.

(d) Defend with courage. Never give an opponent a free and unchallenged chance to play the ball whether it is on the ground or in the air. Above all, never, never give in. There is always a last chance to retrieve an apparently impossible situation. How often have you seen a full back appear from nowhere and kick a fierce shot off the goal line when the goalkeeper seemed hopelessly beaten?

The Front Block Tackle

In Photo 1 the two players are approaching for a block tackle. Notice their balance and concentration on the ball as they move into the tackling position. The contact has been made in Photo 2 (close up Photo 3). Which player is in the stronger position? No. 9 is leaning slightly backwards while his opponent is in a compact and firmly balanced position.

The player on the left of the photograph will win the tackle because he has the best position from which to resist the challenge. Smaller players are often the best tacklers since their lack of height enables them to force taller players off-balance. What does this mean to a tall player if he wants to improve his tackling? He must bend his knees so that he lowers his body position—in other words, while tackling he must try to reduce his own height! Try it yourself.

Photo 1   Photo 2   Photo 3

The Side Block Tackle

This tackle is used when the defender is travelling in the same direction as an opponent who has the ball and when the defender knows that his opponent has not enough speed to get away. In Photos 4, 5, 6 and 7 we see the long stride of the defender (No. 4) which takes his non-tackling foot as near to the ball as possible. Note how his foot, in this case the left, is turned outwards to allow a full turn into the tackle (Photo 5). In Photo 6 we see the pivot which takes place powerfully as No. 4's tackling foot blocks the ball. Once again No. 4 has lowered himself into a strong position in which his knees are bent. In Photo 7 the defender has used his block tackle to force the ball between the opponent's feet and away from him.

Photo 4

Photo 5

Photo 6

Photo 7

The Sliding Tackle

Desperate situations demand desperate measures. The sliding tackle is most often used as a last resort when an opponent is picking up speed with the ball and you know that he will run away from you if he is allowed to continue to accelerate. Since the defender must 'go to ground' in this tackle, success must be one hundred per cent certain and, if possible, the ball should go out of play as a result of the tackle.

The sequence (Photo 8) shows the concentration and determination which must go into the effective sliding tackle. Notice how the tackling leg should be the leg which is farthest away from your opponent. This means that your weight is supported on the near side leg and the near side hand or arm. As the tackling leg and foot swing across your opponent's line of travel the swing must be vigorous to ensure that the ball is played well away to safety and *away from other attackers.* It is no good slide tackling the ball away from one opponent to another. Since you will finish up on the ground you will be as badly beaten as if you had missed the tackle altogether!

Sequence Photo 8

The Sliding Block Tackle

In the sequence (Photo 9) we see a defender sliding into a block tackle. In these circumstances he feels that, while he must slide to reach his opponent, he can obtain a firm holding position rather than having to kick the ball away desperately. In other words, being a good defender he has decided to get the ball (which is what good defending is all about) rather than give it away.

*Sequence
Photo 9*

Intercepting
Meeting the Ball

We have already considered the place of intercepting the ball, before it reaches an opponent, in a back player's duties. Good footballers, whatever their position in the team, *always* move to meet the ball rather than wait for it to reach them. In many ways the basic difference between playing as a schoolboy, youth or amateur, and playing in top class football is the time factor. The higher you go the less the time available in which to use your skill. Professionals must be able to master and control the ball while moving towards it very quickly.

In the sequence (Photo 10) we see the defender moving in front of an attacker to meet the ball and smother it. In this case he is using his chest and stomach to do so. Since he is moving at top speed towards the ball he must be able to relax the parts of his body with which ball contact will be made. He hardly checks his forward speed at all.

Sequence Photo 10

In Photo 11 the defender has used the sole of his foot to smother the pace of the ball. This will be done using one skip step on his left foot. As the ball strikes his studs, his ankle, knee and hip will be relaxed so that they 'give' slightly allowing the ball to be brought under control.

Photo 11

In Photo 12 the defender is demonstrating how to smother the ball while running forward to meet it using his chest.

Photo 12

Volleying

Defenders have little time to clear the danger area when the ball comes to them. Your own penalty area is not the best part of the field in which to show fancy skills. The danger area must be cleared as quickly as possible at all times when opponents are near. In these circumstances the volley clearance kick is very important.

In the sequence (Photos 13, 14 and 15) we see the player concentrating on judging the approach speed of the ball. Note how he has 'coiled' himself by twisting his body from left to right (Photo 13). In Photo 14 he is uncoiling or opening his body as he prepares to volley the ball away to *his* left. See how his non-kicking foot is planted firmly and turned outwards. This foot position will allow him to pivot or turn his body fully in the direction in which he intends to kick the ball. In Photo 15 he has leaned away from the ball in order to get his kicking leg high as he swings through the ball. Look again at the balance and concentration.

Photo 13   *Photo 14*   *Photo 15*

Photo 16

Photo 17

Photo 18

In the sequence (Photos 16, 17 and 18) we can see a defender using the volley technique when the ball is coming directly towards him. In Photo 16 he is judging the final travel of the ball towards his kicking foot. In Photo 17 he is preparing to swing his kicking leg to meet the ball. Notice how power will be developed using a relatively short leg swing and follow through. In Photo 18 we can see the short follow through and, more important, the fully stretched ankle of his kicking leg which will give the player the best possible kicking surface.

Heading

The game of football is developing all the time. New ideas come and go and different teams, through their successes, affect playing fashions and styles from time to time. One simple fact remains, however, and that is that goals are scored when forwards are prepared to show skill and courage in the penalty area when placing the ball past the opposing goal-keeper with foot or head. Modern defensive organisation allows opposing attackers very little time or space on the ground and consequently 'aerial' attackers are more important than ever. If attacking players aim to send clever teasing centres towards goal, defenders *must* develop great skill in judging the danger involved and an equally sure technique in heading clear of goal.

Defensive heading is more a matter of power than placement perhaps but the defender who can head powerfully and accurately not only clears the danger area but sets up counter attacking possibilities at the same time.

Power Heading

Like power in kicking, power in heading is the result of causing that part of your body which makes contact with the ball to be moving as fast as possible as contact is made. This is true of all powerful hitting movements. The head of the club at golf, the face of the racket in tennis and the blade of the bat in cricket. Any energy expended which does not go into achieving this result is wasted as far as power is concerned. A second factor is common to all hitting or striking games. The larger the area with which you strike the ball, the more accurate the kick or hit which results is likely to be. The third factor which is the same in all cases is that you must strike, kick or hit *through* the ball rather than *at* it. This means that, in all cases, where maximum power is required, a follow through must take place.

Heading from the Ground

Power is developed from your legs and feet. A comfortable standing position with one foot in front of the other will allow you to move your upper body forwards and backwards a reasonable distance without over-balancing. As you judge the flight and speed of the oncoming ball your body is bent backwards and, while your full forehead faces squarely towards the ball, it is drawn fully backwards, or cocked, by your neck muscles (figure 23a).

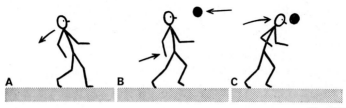

Fig. 23

As the ball reaches a point at which you can move your head forward to hit it so you throw your forehead towards the ball by pushing off your back foot and straightening your body. Your legs throw your hips forward (figure 23b), your hips cause your trunk to move forward and your trunk causes your neck to bring your head forward (figure 23c). Since your head moves last of all the action is very like the action involved in cracking a whip.

Remember what was said about an accurate contact between head and ball? That's right, the largest and flattest part of your head is the front forehead just above your eyebrows and below your hair. It is not only the flattest part of your head, it is also the hardest. Many young players become frightened of heading because, mistakenly, they try to head the ball with other parts of their heads—the side, the back and the top. The result is often painful and this may cause them to go through their football career, even as top class players, with a fear of heading. Develop your heading skill by using your forehead and you will be on the right track. Finally, however fast the ball may be travelling, make sure that *you hit the ball.* If you can avoid it, *never let the ball hit you* by holding your head still and *never* sink your head into your shoulders when trying to head. Your neck is a very good shock absorber but if your head is pulled in by your neck you will have no spring available to take the shock and this can be very painful.

Judgment in heading means that you must watch the ball all the time. Your eyes are well protected by the bony ridge above them so don't be afraid to keep your eyes open.

Heading in the Air

The rules for power heading in the air are exactly the same.

(i) Your head must be moving as fast as possible *as it hits the ball.*

(ii) *Throw* your head towards the ball.

(iii) Strike the ball *with the front part of your forehead.*

(iv) Keep your eyes *open* all the time.

That's fine, you may say, but how is it possible to follow these rules while jumping to head?

In the first place choose a starting position which will be based upon a number of judgments.

(i) At what point in its flight do you think the ball will be dropping low enough to allow you to head it?

(ii) How much run do you need to reach this height?

(iii) How fast do you have to run to get to the ball before your opponent?

Remember these points when we come to arranging practice to improve your heading.

Most players need three or four running paces to jump high. Take off on one foot and use your 'free' leg and both arms by throwing them forward and upwards as strongly as you can to gain 'lift'. Now comes the difficult part. As you take off you have bent your head and trunk backwards. You will find that if, while in the air, you can kick both your heels up behind you, your body will be in the right position. As the ball arrives you jacknife forward throwing your forehead towards the ball and through it.

Fig. 24

The sequence is as in figure 24.

On many occasions during a game the ball will approach you at an angle so that you cannot face the ball squarely. In these circumstances the rules are the same except that you use your neck to turn your head in order to strike the ball with your forehead.

To head powerfully and well clear of your penalty area throw your forehead at the lower half of the ball. By doing this you lift the ball to gain height and distance. If you are in a position to place the ball accurately then you must rise above the ball and head powerfully down through the upper half of the ball.

Skill Practice

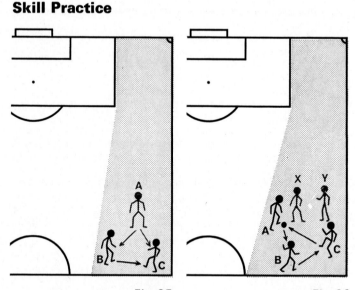

Fig. 25   Fig. 26

in figure 25 player **A** faces an attack by players **B** and **C**. The pitch is the channel shown as a shaded area. The attackers **B** and **C** must try to reach the final area between the edge of the penalty area and the touch-line before they can attack the goal. This will provide good 'jockeying' practice for the defender **A**. If **A** gains possession of the ball or forces it out of the shaded area, **B** and **C** must return to the half-way line and start again.

In figure 26 three attackers **A**, **B** and **C** attack two defenders, **X** and **Y**, to achieve the same purpose as in the previous practice (figure 25). Obviously if **X** and **Y** retreat carefully, covering each other well, they will be in a much better position to challenge for the ball when the attack is forced to play in the narrow 'neck' of the playing channel.

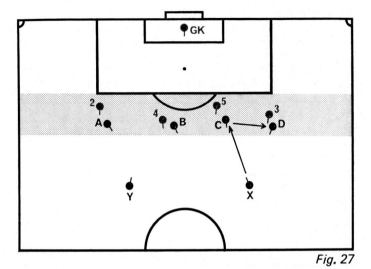

Fig. 27

In figure 27 four backs, Nos. 2, 4, 5 and 3, mark and cover against four attackers, **A**, **B**, **C** and **D** The defending goal-keeper is in position and there are two supporting players for the attack, **Y** and **X**. In the first stage the players 2, 4, 5 and 3, together with the attackers, **A**, **B**, **C** and **D** cannot move outside the shaded area. **A**, **B**, **C** and **D** try to make space for a shot at goal but in addition they can play the ball out of the shaded area back to **Y** or **X** if they wish. Should the defenders be successful in challenging for the ball they will use their goalkeeper in trying to hit a long pass directly into the centre circle.

In the second stage of practice, servers **Y** and **X** can occasionally feed passes over the zone into the penalty area in which case players 2, 4, 5 and 3 together with **A**. **B**. **C** and **D**, the attackers, can attack accordingly.

If we wish to give tackling practice to the backs we can impose certain rules. Reduce the number of attackers to three and require them to make at least five passes in the zone before they can shoot or pass back to the servers **Y** and **X**

Marking

In one half of a pitch there are two full teams dressed in team shirts. Within this area 8 pairs of players, who are responsible for marking each other, can move freely but not into the penalty area or the half of the centre circle. There are two players and the opposing goalkeeper in the penalty area at one end with the other goalkeeper and two opponents in the half centre circle at the other end. In figure 28 black player No. 2 has the ball and will attempt to set up an interpassing movement with any of the 'free' black players who will try to play the ball so that the black goalkeeper can catch it. If the ball is in the possession of the red team they, of course, try to move the ball into the possession of their goalkeeper. A 'goal' is scored when this is achieved. The players in the penalty area and the half circle must not move out of these areas and, of course, other players cannot move into them. If and when the game becomes easy play it with two balls.

Fig. 28

Volley Clearances

In figure 29 three backs are positioned in the goal area. Five feeders take up positions perhaps 30 to 40 yards outside the penalty area and around it. As a ball is lofted into the goal area the three defenders must clear it first time. If an attempted clearance fails to clear the penalty area the four attackers, **A**, **B**, **C** and **D**, are permitted to shoot at goal but they are only allowed two touches of the ball to do so. **A**, **B**, **C** and **D** cannot enter the goal area, while the three backs can only leave the goal area to block a shot. This situation gives effective practice in clearing the penalty area and, if an intended clearance lands at the feet of an attacker in or near the penalty area, as in the game, at least one defender must move out to challenge the attacker quickly in an attempt to block the shot. *Never* allow an attacker a free and undisturbed shot at goal.

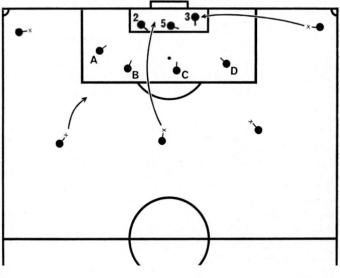

Fig. 29

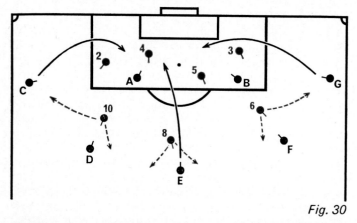

Heading

In figure 30 the four back defenders, 2, 4, 5 and 3, are in the penalty area but *not* in the goal area. The backs are opposed by two attackers, **A** and **B**, who try to score or to put the backs under pressure as they endeavour to head clear. Feeders **C**, **D**, **E**, **F** and **G** interpass to set up lobbed passes into the penalty area and defenders 10, 8 and 6 oppose them. The players who are outside the penalty area are never allowed inside it and the players inside the penalty area cannot leave it. There is no goalkeeper. If a corner is conceded, the corner kick is taken.

Fitness for Backs

The modern game needs speed and stamina of a very high order. All running activities with and without the ball must involve a considerable number of 30 to 40 yards sprints. A player's stamina is improved when he can reduce the amount of rest between each burst of all-out work and increase the number of all-out bursts. Aim to cover about 1,800 yards at top speed in short bursts when you are at peak training level. Occasionally, perhaps once every two or three weeks, substitute hard runs over 300 to 400 yards for the short bursts.

Speed Stamina Circuits (figure 31)

Set up the following activity programme using the football pitch and its markings to help you.

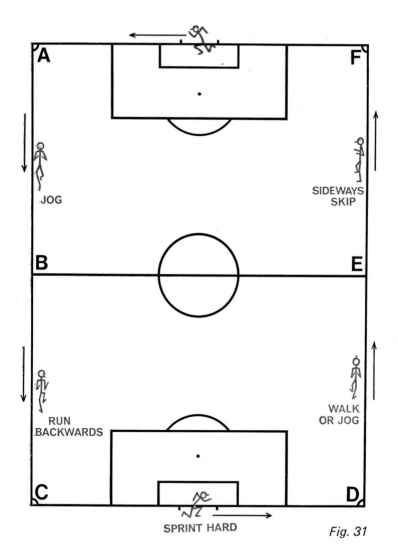

Fig. 31

FIRST TIME ROUND

Jog from A to B. Run backwards from B to C. From C to D sprint as fast as you can. D to E is a relaxing stretch walk or jog, on your toes all the time. Skip sideways from E to F and sprint the final leg from F back to A.

SECOND TIME ROUND

From A with a ball, sprint dribble to a point level with the corner of the penalty area. Back to A as quickly as you can running backwards and pulling the ball along using the soles of your feet. Repeat this activity FIVE TIMES.

Jog slowly in a relaxed way to B. At B perform 20 tuck jumps. Tuck jumps are jumps which have a double foot take off and while you are in the air pull both knees as high as you can, as near to your chin as possible.

From B kick a ball as high as possible to land between B and the penalty area at C. Run after it, control the ball, sprint on and into the field of play. Shoot when you are in the penalty area.

Starting at C move round the outside of the penalty area keeping the ball in the air all the time. Complete one trip around the penalty area and back to C. Jog from C to D.

At D, supporting yourself by placing both hands on the ball, do 4 sets of press-ups. Each set should be made up of five press-ups and they should be carried out as quickly as possible.

At D kick the ball high towards the centre circle, run after it and bring the ball under control before it bounces twice in the circle. As soon as the ball is under control dribble sprint around the outside of the centre circle.

Walk back to point E.

Starting at E move to F keeping the ball in the air by bouncing it continuously on your knees.

As soon as you reach F sprint dribble into the penalty area and shoot for goal.

Walk to point A and repeat the circuit of activities.

All training and practice situations must offer some kind of challenge to the abilities of the player. If training or practice is easy it must be a waste of time. The more realistic the practice is, the better the purpose which it will serve.

In figure 32 the black goalkeeper throws a pass to the full back (black No. 3, top right). The full back runs towards the

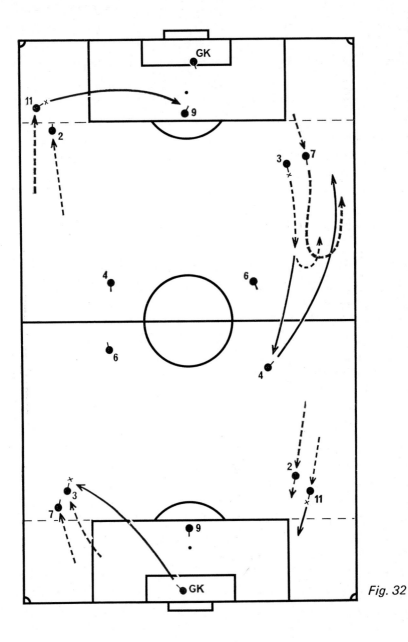

Fig. 32

half way line and while challenged by an opponent, (red No. 7), tries to give an accurate pass to black No. 4. As soon as the pass has been given, No. 7 turns back towards goal to receive a lofted or chipped pass from No. 4. The full back must now turn and sprint after No. 7 who, as soon as he reaches a part of the field level with the penalty area can cross the ball for the waiting centre forward. *Both* full backs, or *all four* for that matter, can be kept busy in this way at the same time.

The modern full back must be:

(1) Quick.

(2) Tenacious.

(3) Skilful.

and (4) Intelligent.

The days when full backs were merely stoppers are gone. Nowadays full backs must be prepared to start attacks, and if possible finish them with an effective scoring shot. In England we have the finest full backs in the world but look how different each one is. There is no set pattern of play for today's full back and there is no longer one type of player who is best suited to this position. A good player is an effective player wherever he happens to find himself on the field of play and remember, practice is the only way to become perfect.

MID-FIELD PLAYERS

CONTENTS

Modern footballers must be good all-rounders. They must have speed and agility, they must master the techniques of all positions, and above all they must be able to 'read' the game.

Players in certain positions will be in contact with play more than others. Mid-field players form the front line of defence. They also provide the link between back defenders and the front players or strikers and they must support and take part in the final attacking movements.

Some mid-field players will be better equipped as 'readers' of the game when their team is trying to regain possession of the ball or working to contain and restrict opposing attacking play. Stiles of Manchester United and Mullery of Tottenham are good examples of this type of player. Others play an important part in setting up the first defensive barrier but are rather better equipped to move forward quickly and move cleverly when their own team breaks out from defence into attack. Martin Peters of Tottenham, Alan Ball of Everton and Bobby Charlton of Manchester United are good examples of forward searching mid-field players.

In figure 1 we can see the positioning of the England mid-field players, Ball (7), Charlton (9), Stiles (4) and Peters (16), as they might have faced an opposing attack during the 1966 World Cup. Stiles, the best defender of the four, moves across the field somewhat behind the other three as the opposing attack switches its direction. This system produces a heavy concentration of players wherever the opposition has the ball and requires a very high rate of work from the 'engine room' of the team, the mid-field players. All the players mentioned have a high capacity for work or running on a football field.

In figure 2 we see how the England mid-field players might break out from defence into attack. Ball and Peters search for advanced attacking positions wherever attacking space might be found. Charlton is renowned for long powerful bursts down the centre of the field as the 'strikers', Hurst (10) and Hunt (8), move out to make space for him and to take defenders away from that part of the field which Charlton attacks so well. Stiles tracks down attacking play from behind, but offers himself as a supporting player whenever the development of play demands it.

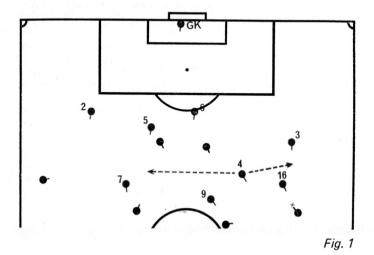

Fig. 1

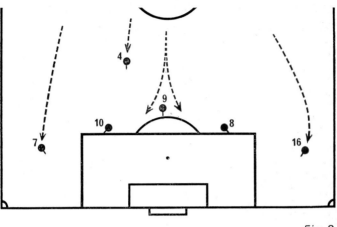

Fig. 2

The grouping of these four players as a unit was probably a key factor in England's World Cup success. Ball and Stiles are quick, aggressive and terrier-like in their play. They give opponents little or no time in which to play. Charlton has all the attributes of a great footballing athlete—technique, enormous acceleration and considerable power of shot in both feet. Peters, by experience a wing half back, has an uncanny ability to 'see' and steal into dangerous forward positions, added to which is the gift for delivering the 'killer' pass with wonderful timing, weight and accuracy. The 'killer' pass is that pass which goes through, over or around an opposing defence and appears, to the defence at least, to be impossible—until it is made!

Recent developments in the game have caused many teams to use four mid-field players as a basis for defence and attack, but some years ago Brazil achieved great success using only two mid-field players. They were required to fulfil the same functions in team play, acting as the first line of defence, linking defence with attack and finally supporting full attacking play.

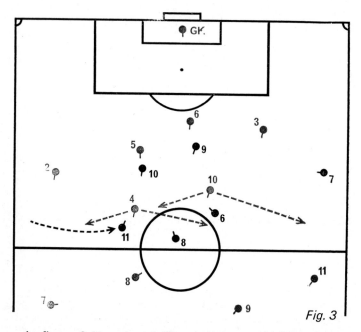

Fig. 3

In figure 3 Nos. 4 and 10 are the two mid-field players, defending in what is known as the 4–2–4 system. In this diagram it can be seen how much work these two players will have to do in attack and defence. The opposing team has withdrawn one attacker (No. 11) to join Nos. 6 and 8 as a third mid-field player. This tactic must place the mid-field unit of two players at a great disadvantage since they will be outrun and will have little time and space in which to act as a link between defence and attack.

Defensive Depth

A mid-field player is responsible for forming the deflection point of defensive triangles. He must be prepared to push forward on to opposing players, particularly when they have the ball or are preparing to receive it. Good defensive organisation shows itself in a series of interlocking triangles. We can see this in figures 4 and 5 where the various defensive triangles are shown in isolation from each other and then related to one another as they will be near the penalty area.

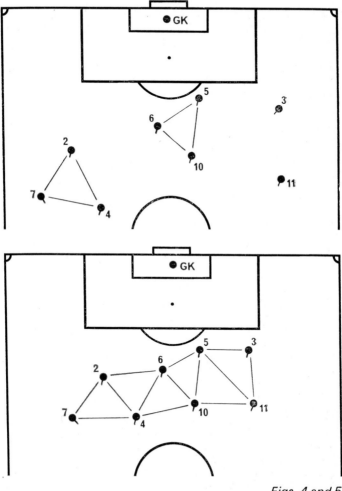

Figs. 4 and 5

Defenders must make opponents play the ball in front of the defence. A defence will be ineffective if opponents are given too much space and time in which to play. Mid-field players are responsible for containing opponents, or presenting them with poor and flat passing angles. In figure 6 the defensive triangle is sound but the defender nearest to the ball, No. 7, is allowing his opponent, No. 10, a chance to play the ball forward easily since he is under no pressure. Both No. 2 and No. 5 dare not mark opponents as tightly as they would like since the ball might be played into space behind them.

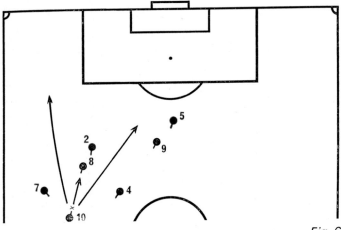

Fig. 6

In figure 7 the defender nearest to the ball has *pushed forward*, thus making the opposing No. 10 choose much flatter passing angles. As a result his two defending team-mates can mark opponents tightly, since there is no danger of a pass being made over their heads. As they force the opposing team to play square across the field in front of them, the mid-field players will produce a 'high pressure' area near and around the ball. This pressure point causes opponents to play their passes hurriedly.

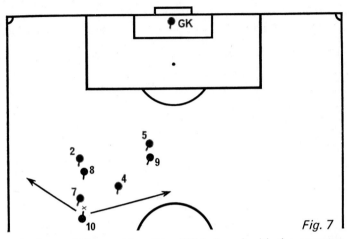

Fig. 7

In figure 8 the attacker (No. 10) is faced with the pressure point made by the opposing No. 8, closely supported by Nos. 4 and 6. If the attacker continues to move across the field, or perhaps to give a pass to his own No. 8, the pressure point may become defender No. 6 or No. 8, supported in the same way from behind.

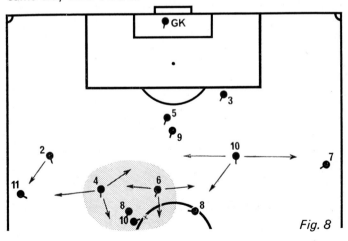

Fig. 8

Pressure points produced in this way show the need for understanding the principle of concentration in defence— *a concentration of defenders in all danger areas.* Defenders also need mental concentration of a high order.

Offering Passes

We have seen how a pressure point is pushed out towards any attacker who is in possession of the ball and towards different attackers as the direction of the attack changes. One of the essential skills which is developed by 'thinking' mid-field players is that of showing or inviting a pass to a certain opponent. This skill demands a fine judgement of how far away from the line of a pass the mid-field player can stand and still intercept it.

In figure 9a the mid-field player, No. 7, has positioned himself close to the line of a pass from the opposing No. 8 to No. 11. He may make an interception, but if he fails he has taken too great a risk since he has given his nearest opponent too much freedom.

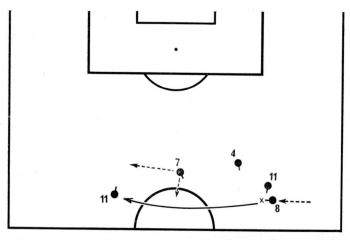

*Fig. 9*a

In figure 9b the mid-field player, No. 7, has positioned himself the same distance from his nearest opponent but where, if he misses the interception, he is still in a position to recover and challenge the opposing No. 11. In both cases, No. 7 could have marked his opponent tightly, which would have prevented the possibility of a pass. But if interception can be made by the mid-field players, an effective counter-attack can be mounted quickly and against a relatively small number of opponents.

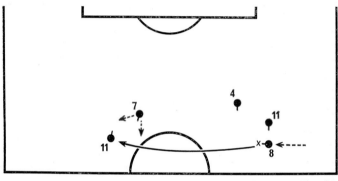

Fig. 9b

Negative and Positive Play

Negative football occurs when a team is never willing to take risks, or when it plays in such a way as to wait for an opposing team to make mistakes. In these circumstances passes are frequently made square across the field or backwards, even when the player on the ball has been given plenty of time and room in which to make forward progress. *Positive football can be seen when a team is willing to risk passes through, over or around opposing defenders which, in turn, means that a team playing positive football must send players forward to look for space behind an opposing defence.* Positive play can, of course, be developed from apparently negative positions if mid-field players are willing to look for forward passes as first choices and if, having given them, the same players are willing to support the strikers and run into attacking space beyond them.

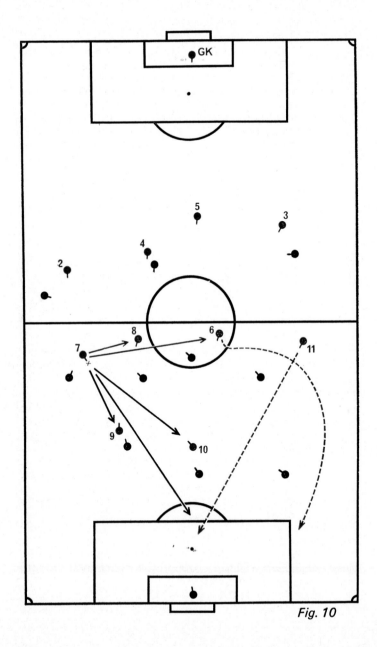

Fig. 10

In figure 10 the red team, although in possession of the ball in their opponents' half of the field, have kept a basic 4–4–2 pattern which is defensive. This will cause a great deal of square passing to develop which may be negative since the object at this stage should be to make quick progress into shooting positions. If No. 7, in possession of the ball, looks for the penetrating pass, perhaps to the feet of No. 9, his pass will cause defenders to be attracted towards the ball. If, at the same time, No. 11 makes a positive run towards and into the penalty area, there is a chance of a break-through. Even more important, No. 6 can leave his mid-field position reasonably safely to begin an 'overlap' run into the space which has been created down the left side of the field.

Some first class teams deliberately change the emphasis in their mid-field unit according to their assessment of the teams against which they are going to play. In figure 11, where the team concerned has a mid-field unit of three players, who happen to be Nos. 6, 8 and 10, we can see the defensive adjustment which takes place when needed.

Both No. 6 and No. 10 are withheld from forward attacking runs to a great extent. They will make themselves available as supporting players, but always from behind and obviously this will increase the safety factor in the team's play. No. 8 will be allowed to go forward on full attacking runs but when his team loses possession of the ball he will be required to take up a position relative to the other two mid-field players as quickly as possible.

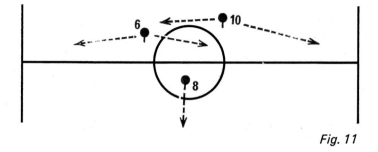

Fig. 11

In figure 12 we can see the mid-field unit as it might be used to emphasise attacking play.

This time both No. 6 and No. 8 will commit themselves to full attacking play when possible. No. 10 will always support them from the back.

In a well coached and skilful team the positions which groups of players take up, particularly in attack, will change constantly. *Variety or change is an important principle of attacking play.* An attack must have *MOBILITY* whereby different players interchange with one another quickly and intelligently. Without mobility an attack loses the important element of surprise and becomes stereotyped and predictable.

Playing Passes into Space

Many people think that good passing in football means delivering passes accurately from one player to another. This kind of judgement is too simple in high class football. Playing to another player's feet is too general a target. We must take into account the following considerations:

Which is the best foot or side to aim for?

A player who has a preference for his left foot will have problems if passes are given towards his right side. This is a vital consideration when he has his back towards the opposing goal and an opponent is close behind him.

Where should the pass be played to?

When a player is tightly marked he has to work hard to dodge his opponent. This involves dodging or dummying one way, to throw his man off balance, and moving quickly in the opposite direction. In this situation a pass played into space will be more helpful to him.

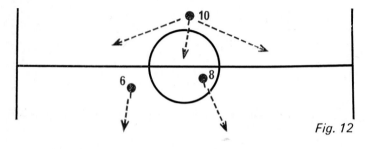

Fig. 12

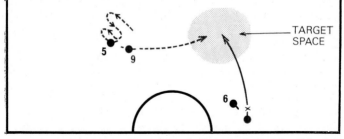

Fig. 13

In figure 13, the striker, No. 9, has performed a 'double dummy' run to take his opponent away from the space into which he wants the ball to be delivered.

How should the pass be given?

The quality of a pass is measured by the ease with which the receiving player can control the ball when it arrives. In most cases this means that the pace of the pass will be 'dying' or 'fading' if it has been delivered with the right amount of weight behind it. Passes which are too heavy are those which receiving players are always fighting hard to catch, or working hard to control.

When should a pass be given?

The timing of a pass is the most difficult aspect. *A pass should be given when the receiving player is in the most comfortable position to receive it.* Too often players who are in possession of the ball give a pass when it suits them to do so. They then blame the 'target' player for not being in position to receive it, forgetting that he has to work hard to make space for himself.

A golden rule in football is: always try to make your team-mates look the best players in the world. If you want to look a good player at their expense then you are a bad player!

Finally, all players must ask themselves these questions when they have made a pass.

What was the pass meant to achieve?

What was in my mind before I gave the pass?

Having given the pass what did I do to help to develop the attack?

Was the pass given for the benefit of the team, or to make me look good?

Useful Practice games to develop passing skill and understanding among two, three or four mid-field players

Attack v Defence

In the early stages of practice the attack will outnumber the defence. As the attack develops understanding and success, defenders are added until, at a very high level of skill, the defence may outnumber the attack.

In figure 14 we are playing 6 v 4 (plus a goal keeper) and we might 'condition' the game so that each attacker *MUST* touch the ball three times at least before he may give a pass. *A 'condition' becomes an extra rule or law to cause a certain emphasis in the game.* 'Compulsory 3 touch' means that a receiving player must bring the ball completely under control before he gives a pass. As a result his passing will be more controlled and careful. If the attack does not make progress quickly we can relax the 'condition', so that it applies only outside the penalty area. This means that if attackers are willing to search for positions inside the penalty area they can earn for themselves the right to pass or shoot first time.

6 v 5 or 6 v 6

Here we will find a need for an interchange of attacking positions. This time we can condition the game so that whenever a player makes a pass he must run to a position beyond the receiver of the pass.

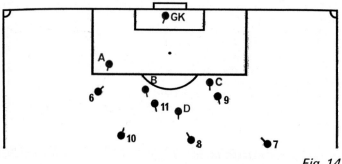

Fig. 14

In figure 15 we can see that if No. 6 passes to the front player, No. 11, he must follow his pass until he takes up a position beyond No. 11. Similarly, in the case of No. 7 passing to No. 9. This kind of practice when used for short periods is useful in bringing about an appreciation of the value of supporting the player with the ball. At the same time players can see the need for continually adjusting their positions relative to each other. *It is often a good idea for a forward to run into a position which a team-mate has just left, particularly when near the goal.*

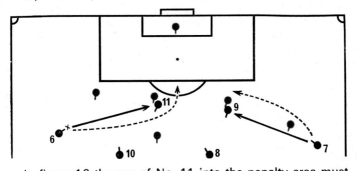

Fig. 15

In figure 16 the run of No. 11 into the penalty area must be covered by the opposing No. 2. If No. 10 can time his run when No. 4 can deliver the ball, the run into the position previously occupied by No. 11 gives No. 4 two positive passing possibilities, both of which may result in a shot on goal.

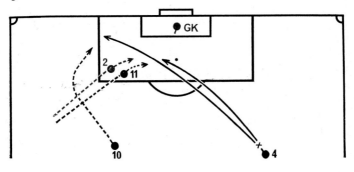

Fig. 16

Sneak Runs

In this practice (figure 17) Nos. 6, 8 and 4 (mid-field players) are not allowed to cross the half-way line unless they are moving to receive a pass. Strikers 9 and 10, and defenders A, B and C, are not allowed to move out of the attacking half although all the attackers can interpass with each other. Attempts are made to develop play so that the attention of all three defenders is drawn away from one side of the field. When this happens, one of the mid-field players will sprint quickly forward to receive a pass. When the defenders gain possession of the ball they can score a 'goal' in two ways:

    (1) By making six uninterrupted passes without using the goalkeeper

or (2) Hitting a pass to the restricted opponents so that they have to move *no more than one step* in any direction to control or catch it.

    As the practice develops, a defender is added and another mid-field player. This time we can allow any two mid-field players to move forward.

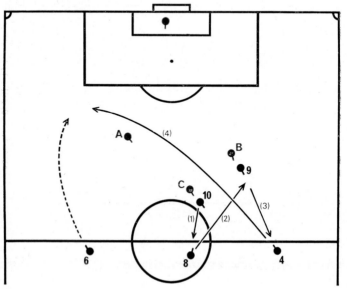

Fig. 1

The Techniques of a Mid-Field Player

The modern footballer must be an all-rounder, capable of playing effectively in any position on the field. Above all, you must understand what is required in any part of the field in the different stages through which a game passes. If you find yourself defending near your own penalty area you must understand how your job will differ from a situation in which you may be defending in the opponents' half of the field. Near your own penalty area you cannot take chances; farther up-field a chance may be worth taking to intercept a pass or to tackle an opponent, since you will have time in which to recover if you make a mistake. Calculating the risk is a matter of skill, judgement and experience.

Control and Pass

Quickness in bringing the ball under close control is an important technique for players in all parts of the field, but it is vital to the mid-field player as he will usually be surrounded by opponents. Having used, perhaps, one movement to control the ball, he must be able to give a pass with his next movement. In many situations the mid-field player will not have time even to bring the ball under control, but will be required to 'lay off' a first-time pass to a supporting player. This means that *the good mid-field player must always have two or three possible passes in his mind before the ball comes to him.*

There are three or four basic principles which you must master if you want to bring the ball under instant and close control. These apply whatever the part of the body with which you wish to control it.

1.   Make sure that part of your body which is to bring the ball under control is in line with the flight of the ball. Move your feet rather than reach whenever you can.
2.   Relax that part of your body which is to be used to stop the ball. If it is your foot, relax your ankle. If it is your head, relax your neck and so on.
3.   Just before the ball strikes, draw the stopping surface away from the ball so that you cushion the impact.
4.   The faster the ball is travelling, the quicker you must withdraw the controlling surface to take 'pace and weight' out of the ball.

When your control is near perfect you should be able to almost 'catch' the ball with any part of your body.

The sequence in the Photos 1, 2 and 3 show a top class player bringing a ball under control with the top of his foot (his instep)—notice the concentration, balance and, above all, his relaxation.

The pass which can be given after the controlling movement has been made may be a short volley (a pass which is given before the ball touches the ground) or a half volley (a pass which is made just as the ball touches the ground).

The short volley can be given in different ways with different parts of the foot.

The short volley lob is used to play the ball delicately over the heads of near-by players. The ball is struck with the instep (the laces of your boot) and the technique involves the knee of the kicking foot only. To volley a pass down to the feet of a team-mate the 'chop' is used (Photo 4). Here we use the inside of the foot which is chopped downwards against the ball. Finally the direction of a volley pass (or any pass for that matter) can be hidden if you can flick a pass, using your ankle only. In this technique the ankle is bent inwards and the foot is flicked outwards at the ball to knock it in the required direction. The ankle is relaxed as much as possible to produce the flicking action.

The half volley pass is struck in the same way as you strike any kind of pass, the difference being that normal passes are hit when the ball is rolling on the ground. The half volley is hit just as the ball makes contact with the ground after it has dropped. This means that the foot must make contact with the ball slightly higher on its surface than would be the case for a normal ground pass. *The half volley, hit first time so that the resultant pass stays on the ground, is one of the signs of a highly skilful passer of a ball.* Even top class professional players have difficulty with this technique. It is valuable because it saves time.

A mid-field player must make many of his controlling movements when moving quickly towards the ball and, frequently, when he is being challenged by one or more opponents. This means that he must be able to relax one part of his body (the controlling part) while working hard with the remainder of his body.

If in doubt, move with speed and determination to meet the ball. This is good advice for any player. When you have got the ball, probably having challenged an opponent for it, you must calm yourself and regain balance and composure to give a pass or make the next move. It is no good getting the ball and then being forced to give a hurried pass. *When you have the ball you control the game.*

Photo 1

Photo 2

Photo 3

Photo 4

Screening or Hiding the Ball

Mid-field is where a great deal of action takes place. A large number of players occupy this area and, as a result, mid-field players must be good at making time for themselves when there doesn't appear to be any. The technique of controlling the ball while keeping your body between the ball and an opponent will allow you to gain time. As he challenges, move your body so that he is always struggling to get round you. In Photos 5, 6, 7 and 8, notice how the player receiving a high ball hides it from his opponent while it is travelling towards him and after he has controlled it. If he is not allowed to see the ball an opponent will have difficulty in tackling for it without committing a foul.

Practice

The smaller the space the better. Mark out a square 10 yards long by 10 yards wide and, keeping the ball in it all the time,

Photo 5

Photo 6

Photo 7

Photo 8

see how many times you can touch the ball without your friend, who acts as a defender, getting his foot to it. Your opponent should try to get into position to tackle for the ball or knock it out of the square. For this practice use a large ball since it will be more difficult to hide.

Try the same thing with the square marked out near to a wall. Throw the ball at the wall; as soon as you do so, your opponent can challenge. Again try to go for a record number of touches. This will help you to develop the technique of receiving a pass and screening in one movement—*difficult to do but if you want to become a high class player you must master it.*

Tackling

All players should know how to tackle, but a mid-field player particularly needs to master the front and side block tackles. Photos 9, 10 and 11 show a front block tackling situation. Watch the following points when you tackle.

Place your standing foot close to but slightly behind the ball. *Never stretch into a tackle unless you have to.* Concentrate on the ball so that your tackling foot strikes into it at the same time as your opponent's.

Put your full weight behind your tackling foot.

Bend your knees. These are the shock absorbers, but they only absorb shock when they are bent. *Tall players must get down to a tackling position.* In Photo 10 the tall player will lose the ball; his feet are too close together and his position is not low enough.

Photo 9   Photo 10   Photo 11

Photo 12

Photos 11 and 12 show ideal positions for the tackling legs and feet. Get your feet right and you will get the ball, but remember, *determination* to win the ball is a big advantage.

The side block tackle is used against an opponent who has gone past you with the ball but who has not done so quickly enough to be out of range. All tackles should be with the purpose of regaining possession of the ball and using it to advantage immediately.

In Photos 13, 14, 15 and 16, the tackling player (No. 4) must work hard to get as near to his opponent as he can. This will allow him to place his standing foot near to the ball (Photo 15), and turn into the tackle quickly and firmly (Photo 16). Notice how, once again, he has adopted a powerful crouching position. *The more erect you stand in a challenge or tackle the easier you will be knocked off balance.*

Tackling Practice

To develop a good position for your feet and to feel how to use your knees as shock absorbers, place a football against a wall or a strong post of some kind. Make sure that the ball is firmly against the wall and swing into the tackle from a standing position. If you strike correctly, the ball will remain wedged between your tackling foot and the wall. If your foot position is wrong the ball will jump away from the wall.

In a small game, perhaps 3 against 3, make a 'condition' that whoever has the ball must *touch* it six times before he can pass. This means that whenever a player receives the ball he must hold it long enough for an opponent to get in a

Photo 13

Photo 14

Photo 15

Photo 16

tackle. Another good practice is for one player to try to dribble past three or four opponents who stand one behind the other ten yards apart. The player behind cannot try to tackle until the one in front has attempted to do so. This is not only good tackling practice, it is also good dribbling practice.

Above all, the mid-field player must be conscious of time since he will rarely have much of it. We have seen how the mid-field area will always have a large number of players in it, with the result that one player receiving the ball may find himself under challenge from all directions. Control must be instantaneous. A mid-field player must use his eyes all the time trying to *see* what is likely to happen in all parts of the field *before* it happens. Many players, even some with great footballing reputations, allow themselves to become 'ball watchers'. This means that they always allow their attention to be drawn in the direction of the ball. For any player who has a defensive responsibility this is dangerous.

In figure 18, where the red winger, No. 11, has the ball, black No. 4 has allowed his attention to be drawn to the ball and has allowed the opposing red No. 10 to run in on goal. In the same way *black* No. 5 has permitted the opposing red No. 9 to escape his attention.

Players who are defending must always be aware of opponents trying to move behind them. Many times on a football field opponents are more important than the ball. *The ball only becomes dangerous when an opponent receives it in a dangerous position.* If the opponent is allowed to move into a dangerous position freely, you are in serious trouble. *'Eyes in the back of your head' is a good slogan for mid-field players.*

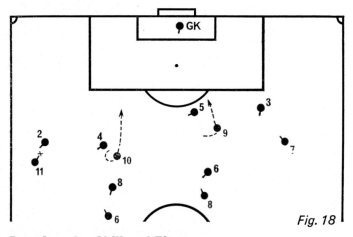

Fig. 18

Practices for Skill and Fitness

Physical fitness without skill is like having a powerful car engine without the car—it will make a lot of noise and smoke but it will not get you anywhere. Skill without fitness is the same as having a Rolls Royce car with no engine. It may look pretty but it won't be any use. Young players must develop skill and fitness at the same time. Even with experienced professional players most coaches spend a great deal of time in trying to invent practices which test both skill and fitness.

We have seen some of the techniques which a mid-field player must master and also the part which he will be required to play in his team's tactical plans, but what are the demands which the game will make on him?

Stamina

Generally speaking he will have to be capable of very quick movement over short distances—say 10–20 yards. This is not enough, however, since the mid-field player is usually in action for most of the game. He must have the *stamina* to maintain these quick bursts for a long period, and for the whole game if he possibly can.

Alan Ball is the man to watch if you want to know how much work a great mid-field player must do. How often does he stand still in a game? How many times does he challenge for the ball and how many times does he touch it? You will find that he works very hard yet touches the ball relatively few times during a match.

1. With some friends, try this practice.

   Mark out a circle 60 yards across with a small circle 5 yards across in its centre (figure 19).

   Players **X** and **Y** start in the small circle. Outside the large circle are six players, three of whom have a ball each. One of these players, perhaps **A**, will shout to player **X**, who will run towards him to receive a pass. **Y** will challenge to try to prevent the pass. When **X** receives the ball he will try to give a pass to any of the players outside the circle who haven't got a ball. When this has been done, both **X** and **Y** must move quickly back to the starting circle. Any of the players outside the circle can then call and the whole thing is repeated.

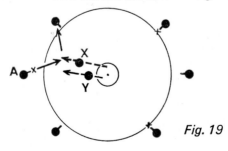

Fig. 19

Each pair of players goes into the circle for 60 seconds and is then replaced by another pair and so on. In 40 minutes each pair will have been in the circle 10 times and will take turns at being the receiver and the challenger. This is ideal stamina training and hard work but then, football *is* hard work. When you find it becoming easy make the time in the circle one-and-a-half minutes and then two.

2. Working with a ball against a wall has always been a popular form of practice and many great players have spent hours playing a tennis ball backwards and forwards against a wall.

    Mark out a small circle, perhaps 3 feet across, ten yards away from the wall. Farther away still make a mark 10 yards from the circle. Place the ball in the circle and get ready to start. Run to touch the ground beyond the mark behind you and return to the ball in the circle. Flick a pass against the wall, control the return and dribble the ball into the circle and repeat the action. Run to the mark, return to the circle, give a pass, control it and so on. One 'trip' is counted each time you return the ball to the circle. How many trips can you complete in two minutes? Have two minutes rest and go again. Do this until you have worked for exactly 20 minutes. What is your total score? Now you have a target to beat. As it becomes easier, work for 30 minutes and then perhaps 40. Stamina work must follow these rules:

    (a) Do a measured amount of work.
    (b) Take a measured amount of rest.
    (c) Repeat for a fixed number of times.

When you want to make the work harder to develop more stamina, do it gradually and in the following way.

  (i) Either increase the measured amount of work in (a) and keep (b) and (c) the same,
 (ii) or reduce the measured amount of rest in (b) and keep (a) and (c) the same,
(iii) or increase the number of times in (c) and keep (a) and (b) the same.

(iv)   Finally, increase both (a) and (c) keeping (b) the same.

This is the basis of 'target training' or 'increased demand' training. All players do it and *it is hard work, but it is the foundation of your football future.*

'Beating the Odds'

1.   In the penalty area or in any area about the same size four players play against two. To score a point the team of four must make eight consecutive passes between them without their opponents touching the ball and the ball must never leave the area. The team of two players score a point if they make three consecutive passes. The test takes place for two minutes, at which time a different pair of players try to beat the odds. What is your record score of points in pairs or fours over a measured period of, say, 24 minutes to start with?

2.   Mark out a small playing area, about 40 yards long by 20 yards wide. The goals can be tin cans or cricket stumps and they are only two yards wide.
      As in figure 20 there are four of these small goals and two players play against one in the area. The two players can only score through goal **A**, but the player who is playing alone can score through any of the four goals. Two points are given for each goal scored and one point is taken away for every scoring attempt which misses. Play for two minutes and change the player who is on his own.

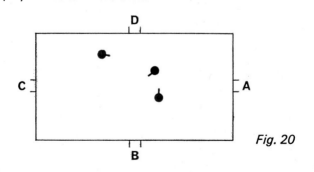

Fig. 20

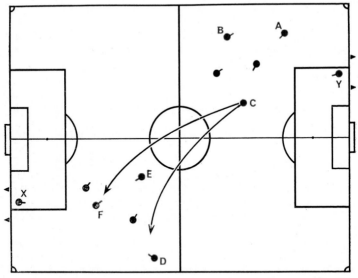

Fig. 21

Switching Play

The mid-field players often control the direction of attacking play. If their positioning is too close to each other, passes become too short and play has no direction or purpose. *If you want to cause difficulty to an opposing defence, changing the direction of attack is important, provided that passing accuracy does not suffer.* How can we set up useful and interesting practice? In figure 21 the field has been 'quartered' by putting in a line down its centre and goals have been marked accordingly. The three red players, **A**, **B** and **C**, will interpass against two defenders and try to deliver accurate cross field passes to attackers **D**, **E** and **F**, who will try to score against the two defenders and the goalkeeper, **X**. When an attack has been completed, **D**, **E** and **F** will now try to play back across the field to **A**, **B** and **C**, who are now attackers trying to score at **Y**. Players will have to work hard to find attacking space and as the defenders are always outnumbered they will have to work hard, although in a relatively small area, to prevent the attacks succeeding.

'Crab' Football

This is a good game for strengthening your stomach muscles, the muscles at the backs of your legs and your arms and shoulders. All the players must take up positions shown in figure 22a. Your weight must be supported on your hands behind you and your feet in front—ONLY! Whenever you attempt to play the ball, or move into another position on the field or court, you must be in the crab position, otherwise a foul is given against you. You score by using your feet or head. Three–six a side on an area 70 feet by 50 feet is excellent. The goals should be 10 feet wide and not higher than 3 feet since the goalkeeper can only play in the same way as everyone else. This is a good game for a gymnasium or small hall.

To change the strengthening effect you can change the position to front support and play ground hand ball (figure 22b). The ball must be played with the fist only and, again, the only supporting positions are the hands and feet. Kneeling or crawling is not allowed!

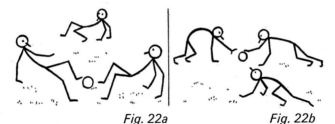

Fig. 22a　　　　　　　　*Fig. 22b*

Shuttle Runs

The course is marked out in a number of stations, usually 10 yards apart as in figure 23. A ball (although any similar object will do), is placed at each 10 yard mark and three should be enough. The players line up in teams of three, one of whom is in the starting circle. On the signal No. 1 in each team runs out and dribbles back one ball at a time until all three balls are in the starting circle. As soon as he touches the starting circle on the last run, No. 2 dribbles the balls out, one at a time, to the three ten-yard marks. When he returns to touch the starting circle, No. 3 does what No. 1 did. The race should last for five 'trips' by each player. The first team to complete the five trips is the winner. It is hard work but it develops the strength and stamina which mid-field players need so much. Any number can be in a team but the more there are the easier it becomes. If there are only three of you, set yourself a fixed number of trips and time your team against a watch. Set yourself improvement 'targets' and try to establish new records.

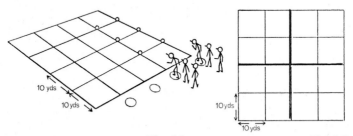

Fig. 23   Fig. 24

Grid Training

The training grid is a useful way of using a small area to obtain the greatest purpose and benefit from training activities. A grid can be as small or as large as you wish but basically it is any area marked out in a series of squares. Generally speaking these squares are 10 yards long x 10 yards wide. Good footballers must become accustomed to playing and working in small spaces; the higher the class of football in which you play, the more this is true. The beauty of a grid, however, is that squares can be joined together to form practice areas of different sizes and shapes.

Figure 24 shows a grid which is 40 yards long x 40 yards wide, divided into 10 yards x 10 yards squares. How many different sized pitches can you find? The red cross will give you four pitches, each of which is 20 yards x 20 yards. Each of these pitches can produce two smaller pitches which are 20 yards long x 10 yards wide, but there are many more combinations which can be used to make different sizes of practice area to suit different needs.

2 v 1

Three players work in one square and two play against one. The ball must never leave the square and the two try to make as many passes as they can without the opponent knocking the ball out of the square. If he succeeds in doing this, his place as an opponent is taken by one of the other two players.

Make the test harder in the following ways:

(i) The interpassing players can touch the ball only with their left foot.

(ii) *Two touch*—the receiving player must touch the ball twice; once to control it and the second touch must be a pass.

(iii) *One touch*—the interpassing players must play the ball first time.

(iv) Passes can be given with the outside of either foot *only.*

(v) To practise the techniques of the game use the extreme corners of the grid as in figure 25. The players must always start in the corners. A throws a high service to **B1** who, if he is trying to improve skill at controlling the ball in the air, must try to bring the ball under control before it touches the ground. As soon as **B** touches the ball for the first time, **C** can run from his corner and challenge for the ball. Meanwhile **A**, having thrown the ball, runs to help **B** and the two try to interpass a set number of times, say five, which is their target. The opponent, **C**, tries to force them to play the ball out of the square or he tries to knock it out himself. If **B** is not so good at controlling he can try it in position **B2**. This means that the opponent **C** has farther to run to make his

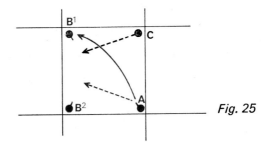

Fig. 25

challenge, and **B** will have more time in which to control the ball. Heading can be practised in the same way. In fact, with a little imagination all the techniques of football can be practised in very realistic ways.

Always give yourself a target and never allow practice to become aimless. Both attackers and defenders must have clear targets and they should score points accordingly. Aimless practice is often worse than no practice at all for it encourages bad playing habits.

Using 2 Squares

Joining two squares together gives us a 'mini practice pitch' 20 yards long and 10 yards wide, which is about right for two against two, three against two or three against three practice. Any practice of a team nature where two or more players are working against two or more players is always improved if we use a small goal to aim at. In figure 26, three players are trying to score against two opponents. It sounds easy, but remember that the two defenders are defending a pitch which is only 10 yards wide. It will be difficult to draw them apart. Players will quickly learn that two opponents can cover each other well until one or two of the attacking group move forward, at which time the attackers must be marked—otherwise they may score. If **C** and **B** go forward to **C1** and **B1**, the two defenders, **X** and **Y**, must try to cover each other while marking **C** and **B** as much as they can. If they mark tightly they will leave space between them. If they cover each other they must leave **C** and **B** free to some extent. To give **C** and **B** practice in finding space in which to receive

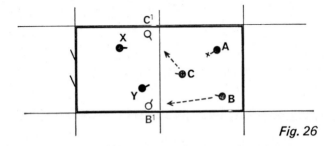

Fig. 26

passes we could restrict **A** to playing in the square farthest away from goal. He can receive passes and give passes but he cannot leave his square. **C** and **B** must now work hard to make room for themselves. If the defenders **X** and **Y** get the ball, their target may be to try to 'hit' **A** with a pass. This will make **C** and **B** aware of their attacking duties and also of their defending duties when they have lost the ball.

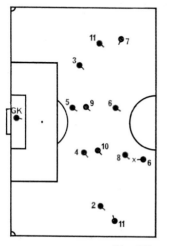

Fig. 27a

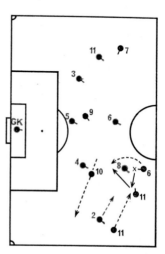

Fig. 27b

Making and Using 2 against 1 Positions

All players at all times should aim to make a situation where two of their team are playing against one opponent. In figure 27a all the attackers are well marked and black No. 6, who has the ball, will have difficulty in making progress. In figure 27b his winger, No. 11, has moved quickly towards him and for a brief moment they have a two v one situation against the opposing red No. 8. Of course the red defender No. 2 will attempt to interfere, but if black No. 11 moves quickly, without showing what he is going to do, his defender will be left two or three yards behind. In this situation black players No. 6 and No. 11 might use a 'wall' pass to get past the nearest defender.

The Wall Pass

This is very commonly used in all classes of football to get behind an opponent in two passes.

In figure 28 No. 6 moves towards the defender No. 8, threatening to dribble past him to the right. In the meantime No. 11 has taken up a position where he can, for a moment, stand still facing his team-mate where it is easy for No. 6 to pass to him. When the pass is given, No. 11 gives a first-time return pass behind the opponent which No. 6 can take in his stride. No. 6 is 'bouncing' the ball off No. 11 as if he is a wall.

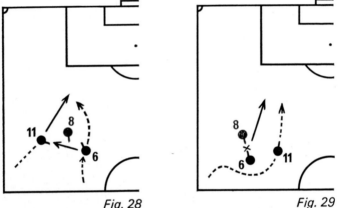

Fig. 28   *Fig. 29*

Overlap Run

In the same situation, No. 11 might run behind No. 6.

In figure 29 No. 11 has run into position for a wall pass, but the opposing No. 8 has positioned himself to stop it. Continuing his run, No. 11 moves behind No. 6 and then 'bends' his run in a forward direction—at which time No. 6 pushes a pass beyond the defender.

There are many ways in which you can exploit the two-against-one position. All of them depend upon:

   (i)   *When* you run into position.

  (ii)   *How* you run into position—the extent to which you can hide your intentions.

 (iii)   *How* you deliver the pass—a pass which is too heavy will make the receiver have difficulty in controlling it. A pass which bounces unnecessarily will also make the ball difficult to deal with by the receiver. Even a pass which is given carelessly, perhaps to the receiver's worst foot, will not help him to help you. Good passing involves a great deal more than accuracy.

Passing is a question of players making the correct angles to a certain extent and, since mid-field players tend to be in the thick of play a great deal, they must think in terms of making angles with other players all the time.

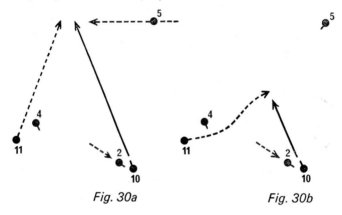

Fig. 30a   *Fig. 30b*

In figure 30a the attacking forward (No. 10) has made a good position for giving a pass inside the defender No. 2. No. 11 has gone on a long forward run making a very narrow passing angle for his partner. The defending No. 5 will certainly cut off the pass, always assuming that No. 11 beats the opposing No. 4 on what will be a long run.

In figure 30b, No. 11 has cut across field giving a much better passing angle for No. 10. He does not have to run so far, but he is running into a much more dangerous position. No. 10's pass is shorter and the opposing No. 5 cannot be so sure of what to do with the certainty of getting the ball.

In a similar way a player who wishes to receive the ball can open up a better passing angle for the player on the ball.

In figure 31a black No. 8 is in a position to give a through pass to the forward player No. 9. The judgement of the pass has to be nearly perfect since the forward player's run to receive it is very close to the line of the pass, thus making No. 8's passing angle very narrow.

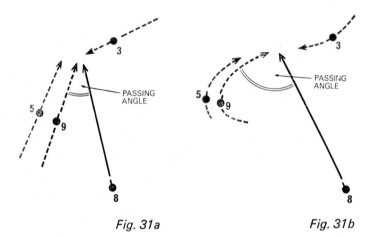

Fig. 31a   *Fig. 31b*

In figure 31b the forward player No. 9 has moved away from the line of No. 8's pass and then returned. This wide run has created more space into which the pass can be made. In figure 31a No. 8 has to judge his pass to avoid interception by two red opponents No. 5 and No. 3. In figure 31b he has the passing angle which will allow him to give the pass so that only No. 5 can challenge for it—if he is quick enough!

Finally, of course, the player with the ball can make his own passing angle better.

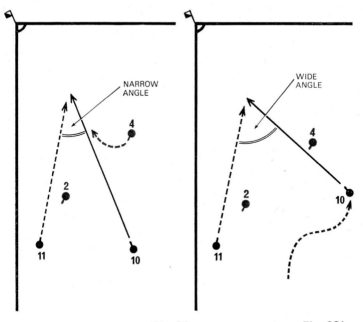

Fig. 32a   *Fig. 32b*

In figure 32a No. 10 can give a very good pass through the two red defenders, but it will have to take into account the difficulties for No. 11 in receiving it as he will be challenged by one or two players. Probably the opposing No. 4 will intercept the pass.

In figure 32b the forward player No. 10 has moved in field away from the player on the wing. This has caused two things to happen. First the covering defender, No. 4, will have moved in the same direction to some extent and so away from his covering position. Second, the passing angle has been widened. Not so easy now for red No. 4 to cut the pass off!

Personal 'Target Training'

Many players have to train alone, or in very small groups and we find that making this kind of training interesting and worthwhile is very difficult unless training targets are used.

'Training Targets' are set amounts of work and they are measured by the *number of times* you can do an activity, or the *time* it takes you to do a set piece of work.

As a simple example, if a part of your training is aimed at improving your ability to jump off two feet, you will *practise* jumping off two feet. But how many times should you practise, how high should you jump, and how long should you take about it?

Stand against a wall, jump off two feet to touch the wall with your hand as high as you can. Make a mark on the wall three inches below the point where you touched. This is your *Height Target*. Now jump to touch the wall above this mark as fast as you can *until* you are unable to reach the mark. How many times did you jump? That is your *Repetition Target*. How long did it take you to do this? A second hand on a watch will tell you and this is your *Time Target*. To increase your targets you:

   (i)   Give yourself more jumps to do at the same height and in the same time,

  (ii)   give yourself less time to do the same jumps and at the same height,

 (iii)   give yourself more height to jump for the same number of jumps and in the same time.

You can see that we have either increased the height or increased the number of times we jump or decreased the total time. We have changed one thing at a time to make the training harder but not all three.

Let's have a look at some simple and useful 'Personal Training Targets'.

Hopping Shuttles

Mark out a 10 yard 'course'. Place a ball behind the starting mark.

   (i)   Hop to the 10 yards mark on one leg and hop back on the other.

(ii)   Dribble the ball to the 10 yards mark and leave it there.

(iii) Hop from the 10 yards mark to the start and back again.

(iv) Dribble the ball back to the starting mark and leave it there and REPEAT.

A 'Training Trip' will be 20 yards of hopping plus the 10 yards of dribbling.

Your target to begin with can be 10 'Trips' and when it becomes easy begin to make the target more difficult. In the example we used height, in this case it will be distance.

This will improve your leg strength and stamina.

Beetle Walk
Over the same course but start with the ball in front of you while you support yourself on your hands and feet (figure 33).

Using one hand only, dribble the ball to the 10 yard mark and back again. Leave the ball and run to the 10 yard mark and back. That is one Training Trip. Your target may be five trips, but change it when necessary as before.

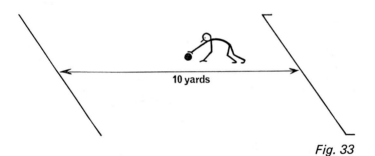

10 yards

Fig. 33

Roll and Run
Using the same course, sit cross legged with the ball in front of you. Throw it up, get to your feet without using your hands, and control the ball with your chest, your head, your thigh or your instep, depending on what you are weakest at. Catch the ball off your chest and, while holding it, do a

forward roll. Then, carrying the ball, run as fast as you can to the 10-yard mark and repeat the activity at that end. Start off with a target of 20 trips.

Many kinds of activity can be used in this way. Using a ball makes things interesting, but always try to include a 10-yard sprint and remember easy targets do not help you or your football.

Run and Pass

Mark a target area on a wall, say 3 yards wide and 2 feet high. Place a ball five yards away from the wall in a chalk circle. Now make a mark 10 yards from the chalk circle.

Run to the ball, pass accurately at the target on the wall. Collect the rebound and replace the ball in the circle. Turn and run to the back mark (10 yards behind the chalk circle) and repeat. Do this at top speed but remember, your pass must be controlled and accurate. If it is not, you will only have to fetch the ball each time and this will spoil the training. Set yourself a target of 20 trips to begin with. If you want to make it harder reduce the target area as your accuracy improves. This activity will show how necessary it is to be able to control yourself and the ball while working hard.

STRIKERS

CONTENTS

Attack is the best form of defence' sounds attractive but it is only half true. Attack *is* the best form of defence when you have a sound defence which is not under pressure. Football is the greatest spectacle in sport when attack and defence are reasonably balanced. From time to time defensive play will appear to dominate the game, but goal scorers will still provide the excitement which is so much a part of football.

In the past, goal scoring really meant finishing off the attacking movements created by other players. The big courageous centre forward took on the equally formidable centre halfback, while wing forwards attempted to get around the opposing full backs and provide centres for the centre forward to 'strike' home with head or foot. Modern tactics and systems of play rarely allow the man-against-man situation to occur. Defence in depth, with highly organised systems of cover, seldom permits an attacking player the luxury of using his skill or courage against one defender. Increasingly, the front attackers or strikers have to work very hard to create space for themselves in a well co-ordinated way. They will also often be required to put opposing back defenders under pressure. Much of their play will be for the benefit of other players, but that has always been the basis of sound team play. Let us look at the changes which have taken place in team systems of play and the tactical use of players during recent years.

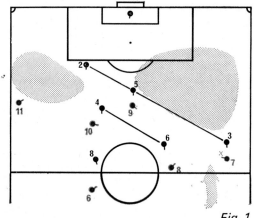

Fig. 1

Pivoting Defence

In figure 1 we can see the basis of the pivoting defence as it existed throughout English football for twenty or thirty years. The five defenders, Nos. 2, 3, 4, 5 and 6, swung or pivoted on the centre half (No. 5) according to the direction of the attack. In this diagram the defence has swung to cover against the threat of an attack developing on the opposing right wing. If an attack were to develop along the opposing left wing the swing would take place towards it with the left back (No. 3) swinging round to cover his centre half (No. 5).

As the diagram shows, the basic idea of the game required one defender to accept a responsibility for one attacker and for covering his nearest team-mate in defence. This is all very well while attackers stay in the same part of the field the whole time. When they begin to interchange positions and still support each other, defensive problems occur.

In figure 2, rather than merely remain as a spectator on the left wing, No. 11 has moved right across the field to produce a situation in which the attack outnumbers the defence. The centre forward, No. 9, has also moved in a similar way while No. 10 has attempted to draw the attention of the central and covering defenders.

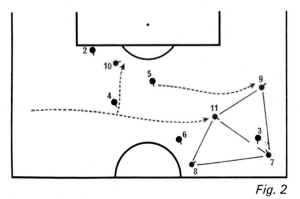

Fig. 2

Sliding Defence

Rather than give opposing forwards the freedom which the slow and cumbersome pivot defence gave, defences became organised so that individual defenders were able to move across the field to shadow the movements of interchanging forwards. This meant that a defending team always needed an extra defender. A space defender, in fact, to fill any gaps which might be created.

In figure 3 the six defenders have been organised to form two lines of three. Within the basic group of 6 the players slide across the field to face the attacking threat and they will always try to form triangles with each other. Near the opponent with the ball the triangles will be quite tight. Further away the triangles will be fairly loose. As danger threatens they will tighten up again. This is the foundation of defensive depth.

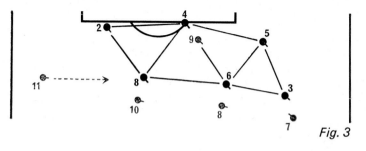

Fig. 3

In figure 3 the attacker, No. 11, is in an orthodox wing position. If he moves across the field he will find himself *'collected'* by whichever defender happens to be free at the time. Attackers increasingly find themselves faced with the double-bank defensive system with eight players making up the 2 banks (figure 4). Variations on these systems also involve a 'free' defender or 'sweeper' behind the back defenders (figure 5) and less frequently a 'free' defender or 'screen' player in front of the back defenders (figure 6).

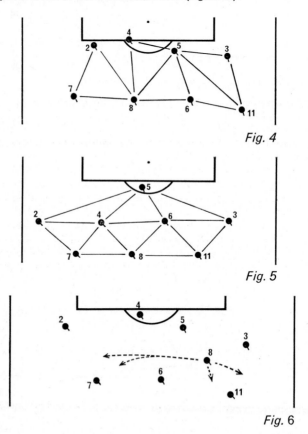

Fig. 4

Fig. 5

Fig. 6

These players — the 'sweeper' or the 'screen' — provide extra insurance against danger wherever the ball happens to be. They shadow the movement of the ball across the field and produce very tight defensive organisation wherever attacking progress is attempted. In addition, if any attacker tries to move into a dangerous position within the defence or towards goal, the 'sweeper' or the 'screen' 'collects' him so that another defender cannot be drawn out of position.

From this brief consideration of the organisation of teams within various systems of play, certain basic ideas emerge which will help the striker to be a better player.

Marking

A forward will find himself marked tightly and watched carefully if he takes up a position near his opponents' goal. Defending players have two vital duties; to *mark* dangerous opponents and to *cover* their own players who are marking dangerous opponents. A forward who moves away from his opponents' goal to take up position will usually find himself not so tightly marked.

The questions to be answered are:—

1. Should the striker try to get into a dangerous position and accept the fact that he will be tightly marked and covered?

   or

2. Should he move into positions in which he will not be so tightly marked because his opponents consider these positions to be less dangerous or not even dangerous at all?

   or

3. Can he move into position in such a way that he will be less tightly marked *and* in a dangerous position at the same time?

If he can regularly achieve a successful answer to question 3 he is well on the way to becoming a great player.

In figure 7, red 9 has the choice of movement in many directions. Whatever he does he can be tightly marked by black 4. Black 5 can still cover the dangerous central part of the field. If No. 9 stays in his central attacking position he will at least collect' the close attention of both the opposing defenders Nos. 4 and 5.

In figure 8 the red No. 9 has moved away from his tightly marked central position and he has been allowed to do so by the opposing No. 4. Why? Because any one of three defenders — No. 4 himself *or* No. 8 *or* No. 6 — can mark him when the need arises. No. 9's new position is causing the defence no problems at all.

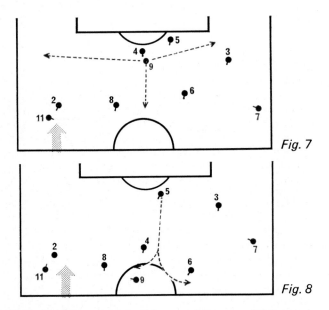

Fig. 7

Fig. 8

In figure 9 as the attack builds up red 9 moves into a position wide of the dangerous central position. If the timing of the pass is right and No. 9 takes his run back into the central position correctly, he may regain his central position at the same time as the ball arrives and cause the covering defender No. 5 a great deal of worry.

If we can involve another striker in the movement at the same time (and this is where planning and coaching come in) we have the foundation for very successful attacking play

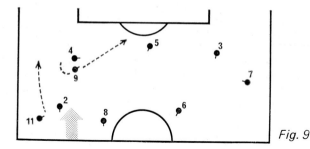

Fig. 9

For example, if, as No. 9 begins his run into a central position, No. 11 can turn and run up the wing, the player with the ball has two choices for a successful and dangerous pass.

A striker must be prepared to run frequently when his effort will not cause him to receive the ball but *will* allow a team-mate to receive it. This skill is known as 'moving off the ball' or 'decoy running'.

In the 1966 World Cup Hunt was a very important player to England, not so much for what he did when he got the ball but far more for what he did in making space for Hurst. Both players were basically right footed and both preferred to move to the right when receiving the ball so that they could control, dribble, pass and perhaps shoot using their better foot. But look what would happen, in figure 10, if they had done so. It would not be a matter of only two people running into the same space but four — Hurst (No. 10) and Hunt (No. 21) *and* two opponents, together with a covering player when England played against West Germany. In this situation, and for the good of the team, Hunt volunteered to run left which meant that he had to accept many passes which

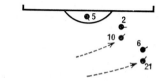

Fig. 10

arrived on his left. Look what problems his unselfish run creates for defenders in figure 11. Hurst and Hunt have 'split' the two marking defenders and taken them into positions where they cannot help each other. In addition, they have created space for the long run of perhaps Charlton (No. 9) into the dangerous central position — the position in which he is most dangerous. This is a perfect example of unselfish running for each other by great players.

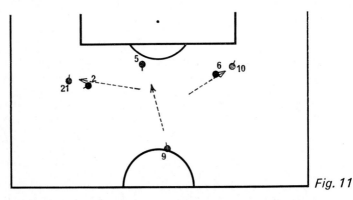

Fig. 11

There are many ways in which two or even three strikers can move to help each other.

In figure 12 both red 9 and red 10 *want* to be tightly marked before a pass is likely to come. It will help them! As the ball is played towards No. 9 he moves to meet it and tries to flick or deflect the ball behind the opposing No. 6. Red 10 will try to turn quickly and gain a surprise advantage on the opponent who is marking him. If the opponent marking him does not follow, red 9 will hold the ball, turn and attack the defence himself.

In figure 13 the two strikers cross over during their runs into position. No. 9 can receive the ball himself or the ball may be delivered into the space behind him. This is the space which No. 10 aims to run into.

If you were a player with the ball, on the same red side and with time to hit a good pass, which red player would you aim for? Better still, which space would you aim for? Red 10 is the player moving into the most dangerous space and he would be the first choice target for your pass.

In figure 14, red 9 and 10 have gone as far upfield as they can and they know that they will be tightly marked. Indeed

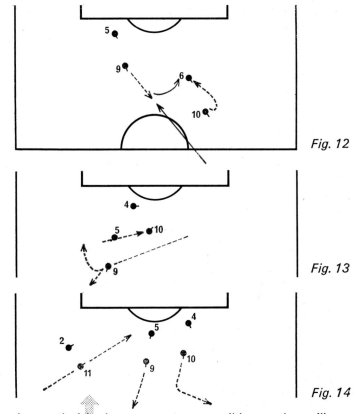

Fig. 12

Fig. 13

Fig. 14

they hope to be! As they run to meet a possible pass they will make space behind their opponents into which perhaps their winger, red No. 11, can move.

These are movements which are often planned and practised in top class football. There are certain rough rules which you can apply.

In figure 15, *your* attacking half of the field has been divided, roughly, into fifteen areas. The number in each area indicates how important it is, generally speaking, compared with other areas. Low numbers show the most dangerous areas and so on.

1. If you are a real striker, if your team expect you to create trouble and score goals, *you must aim to stand in or move into the low-number areas. The high-number areas are not for you except on a few occasions during a match.*

2. *If one of your team mates leaves a low-number area for a relatively high-numbered area you must move into his place* — if you can. You should move just after he has, because his movement may have taken a defender away and he will have created space for you.

3. *Whenever there is a chance of a pass coming, look for the space behind defenders* rather than in front of them. In the numbers plan those dangerous spaces behind defenders will be numbered from (1) to (8) — low numbers again.

4. If you cannot take up a position which is dangerous *or* which will allow a team-mate to move into a dangerous position, *move to support the player who has the ball.* At least this will give your team a chance of keeping possession of the ball. To give the ball away is the worst crime in football.

Young players often hear people (who should know better) continually shouting at them to move about on the field.

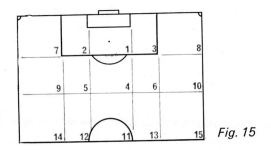

Fig. 15

There is no point in strikers moving about merely for the sake of moving. In fact, for most players, particularly strikers and mid-field players, there are often good reasons for standing still. If you are being tightly marked in a game, try standing absolutely still for, say, 30 seconds — and that's a long time in a football match. You may be surprised at how worried your opponent becomes. In England most players are encouraged to do too much running. Run by all means but make sure that you have a good reason for doing it!

Shooting

A striker must have the ability to put the ball in the back of the net. This is not only a matter of skill in hitting the ball with head or foot; it involves courage, control and optimism. A great striker must think positively: the possibility of missing the goal should not cross his mind, or he will begin to play badly. If he fails he should look forward with confidence to scoring with his next shot.

Scoring is not merely a matter of banging the ball; good goal scorers rarely strike the ball unnecessarily hard. Their shots represent *controlled* power rather than mere force. Wild attempts to burst the net probably mean inaccurate contacts between your foot or head and the ball. These shots are more dangerous to the crowd behind the goal than the goalkeeper. A goalkeeper must be courageous and, since he will frequently challenge a striker for the ball, the striker must show the same determination. Above all else he must have the courage to keep on trying because he is the inspiration of the side. A team playing badly gets an enormous boost from the efforts of a centre forward who never stops trying. He must have courage, control and optimism in these striking positions.

Shooting on the Run

In modern football the striker rarely has the opportunity to produce a long run on goal to shoot. More often he can expect perhaps five to ten yards at the most during which he can move with the ball and shoot.

Shooting Angle

The natural swing of your leg when you kick or shoot is slightly across your body. This enables you to hold a well balanced position; it also means usually that if you are shooting right-footed, the ball will travel from right to left. In figure 16 the centre forward, No. 9, has approached the opposing goal square to the front. The goalkeeper has narrowed both shooting angles (shaded areas) and if No. 9 is right-footed he has given himself target space **A** to aim at. A target perhaps only 3-4 feet wide. If he can swerve the ball by hitting across it with the outside of his right foot he may be able to hit target space **B** but both target spaces are too narrow for safety.

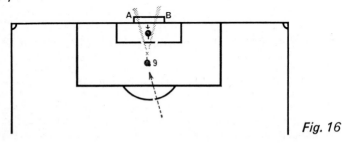

Fig. 16

In figure 17 the player has moved to the right of the penalty spot to give himself a better chance to use the natural swing of his right leg across his body. He has opened up the target space **A** and deliberately allowed the goalkeeper to close up target space **B** almost completely. Making the best shooting angle in these circumstances is a battle of wits be-

Fig. 17

tween the goalkeeper and the centre forward. Make *your* mind up early. If you delay you will find the goalkeeper forcing you to do something you don't want to do. That's what he's there for!

The problem now, apart from getting the ball past the goalkeeper, is to ensure that you do not 'pull' the shot outside the target space. In the case of a right-footed player your left side and left arm will control the direction of your shot. The more your chest is facing the goalkeeper before you strike the ball, the more likely it is that your shot will be 'pulled' from right to left. As your kicking leg swings, throw your left arm across your body or hold your left shoulder towards your target (photos 1 and 2). When you next miss the goal by shooting wide try to remember in which direction your left shoulder was pointing.

The opposite applies for left-footed players.

The position of your foot is shown in photo 3. Notice how the ankle is stretched to give a nearly flat hitting surface for your foot. The more your toe points forward underneath the ball, the more you will lift it off the ground. Keeping the ball low is important.

Photo 1

Photo 3

Photo 2

133

Most goalkeepers are better at getting up than getting down and many goalkeepers do not find it easy to get down quickly.

Photos 4, 5 and 6 show the ideal positions for a low shot. Notice where your knee should be as your foot strikes the ball in photo 5. Notice the fairly low follow-through after the ball has left your foot in photo 6 and see how this player has kept his head down *all* the time. He knows that he has hit the ball well. Too many players want to see the ball in the net before they have kicked it. Keep your head down and look at the ball. The roar of the crowd will tell you if it has gone in or not!

We have seen how to control height and direction but how do we develop a *powerful* accurate shot?

First your leg swing must be a long one which means that your last stride before kicking must be a long one. This allows you to have a high back lift (photo 7). As you swing into the kick, your knee straightens very quickly and powerfully (photo 8) until it follows through towards the target (photo 9). Notice how the player leans away from the ball and, once again, look at the position of his head.

Many players lean away from the ball and to the side in order to develop the long leg technique. You can certainly produce a powerful shot this way but it does not give you any choice of action — the ball must be struck with the inside of your instep and, in the case of a right-footed player, the ball will travel from right to left. When you shoot without leaning away from the ball it is difficult to use a long leg swing to give power: you use the muscles at the front of your thigh to straighten your knee quickly as your foot makes contact with the ball. The technique appears to be more of a stabbing action. It is used a great deal when you find yourself in a shooting position surrounded by opponents and have no time to set yourself for a long swing at the ball. Since the ball is close to your non-kicking foot as you strike it, you will find it possible to change the direction of your shot by altering the position of your kicking foot. This means that the opposing goalkeeper cannot decide, until the very last moment, in which direction the shot will travel.

Photo 4   Photo 5   Photo 6

Photo 7

Photo 8

Photo 9

In photo 10 you can see how the kicking foot, when the ankle is turned inwards, will cause the ball to swerve from left to right. This is because the foot moves across the ball as it strikes, causing the ball to spin and thus, when it is in the air, to swerve. In photo 11 the foot strikes from a central position behind the ball, moving outwards, with the result that swerve will occur in the opposite direction. Look at the diagrams. The foot position in photo 10 will cause the shot to travel as in figure 18. The foot position in photo 11 will cause the shot to travel as in figure 19.

Photo 10   Photo 11

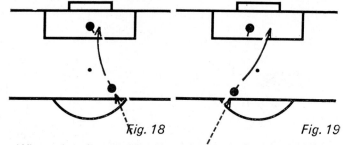

Fig. 18   Fig. 19

When shooting, make your mind up early and then concentrate on striking the ball cleanly and accurately. If you hit the ball where it needs to be hit, the accuracy of your shot is guaranteed. Strikers who dither and change their minds rarely score; the sign of a great goal scorer being out of form is that he seems to be unsure, trying too hard to make his shot certain and taking too long about it. A player who gets a shot in and misses can be forgiven. A player who takes so long about shooting that the ball is taken away from him cannot.

Strikers must be capable of shooting accurately when the ball is bouncing awkwardly and coming to them at different heights and angles. This means that they must be good at volleying the ball, particularly when turning. In photo 12 notice how the player leans away from the ball in order to be able to lift his shooting knee as high as possible. Many players actually fall away from the ball as they shoot in this position. In order to develop additional power the forward will occasionally turn his back on goal in order to get in a full turn of his body as he shoots. The main kicking power will come from the fast straightening of his knee as his foot makes contact with the ball. Notice in the photograph how the player concentrates on striking the ball accurately and cleanly. The spectacular overhead shot is only a development from the principles involved here. The striker has his back toward goal and falls toward it in order to lift his shooting leg high enough to keep the ball on target.

Photo 12

Controlling the Ball, Passing and Shooting

Strikers are usually marked tightly and, as a result, they must develop skill in controlling the ball and shooting or passing in one movement. Other players may often find it difficult to give a well-judged pass to the striker and he may have to accept the ball in very difficult circumstances. Even so he must aim to control the ball perfectly with only one touch.

The player in photos 13, 14, 15 and 16 is controlling the ball and hiding it or screening it from his opponent at the same time. A difficult technique but an important one. Notice his concentration and relaxation but, most importantly, notice how close to his feet he keeps the ball.

Photo 13

Photo 14

Photo 15

Photo 16

In photos 17, 18 and 19 we see a player controlling the ball with his chest and shooting on the volley.

The striker will have little time in which to make up his mind and little room in which to play. Make your mind up early and concentrate on what you are doing all the time. Opponents are there to put you off — ignore them!

Photo 17

Photo 18

Photo 19

Heading

A striker must expect to receive passes at all angles and at different heights. It is obviously a great advantage if he is good with his head and there are many different forms of heading in attack. Some involve great skill, some involve considerable ability to jump high to head, others involve courage but all require:

(a) *Determination to get to the ball first.* and
(b) *Timing the run or jump which will enable you to get to the ball first.*

Let us examine some of the ideas which are used to create chances for successful headers.

Far Post Positions

When using high crosses players should aim for a part of the penalty area and not for a particular player's head. Generally speaking the area which will cause the greatest difficulty to a goalkeeper and other defenders is beyond him.

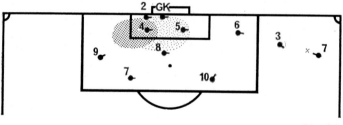

Fig. 20

In figure 20 we can study the heavy disposition of defenders to face the possibility of a high cross from black No. 7. The fully shaded area covers that part of the field which defenders will have difficulty in covering. The position shown by black No. 9 is where a striker who is a good header of a high pass might begin his run in to meet the ball. The area which is partly shaded allows for a cross which is less than perfect but which can also be attacked by No. 9 if he can adjust the speed of his run. No. 7 on the black side aims to drop the ball in the shaded area. No. 9's responsibility is to arrive in that area at the same time as the ball.

As in all playing movements and tactics, each player requires a great deal of help from other players. How can other players help No. 9 in the situation illustrated in figure 20?

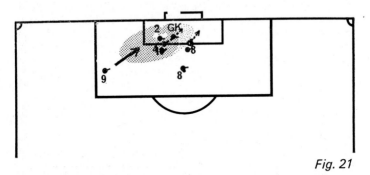

Fig. 21

Look at the diagram and ask yourself: 'If I am No. 9 which opponents are in my way?' Obviously the red players Nos. 4, 5 and 8 since they are near the target area if not actually inside it. Can we move them? Only if we put attackers nearby to attract their attention. In figure 21 black forwards 8 and 10 have taken up positions very close to red defenders 4 and 5. They have moved to invite close attention from these opponents. As the ball is about to be crossed they move towards goal attempting to draw the two red defenders with them since the defenders do not know where the ball is intended to drop. The area which is the real target area has now been opened up (figure 22).

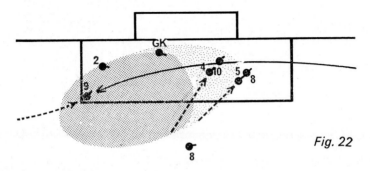

Fig. 22

We can also try to clear another danger area in which headers are often successful, the near post area. In figure 23 both the black attackers Nos. 9 and 8 will move into the target area (shaded) before a crossfield pass or centre looks possible. They will then move out of this area and will be marked closely by the red defenders Nos. 5 and 6. As the centre is kicked, black No. 9 will turn and move quickly for the centre which is aimed to drop by the near goal post. He may flick the ball into goal or knock it over his own head for another attacker to strike at goal. Once again the problem for the player who has to centre the ball has been simplified. We have given him an area to aim for rather than one particular player's head. And, of course, the area presents a much larger target.

To be successful as a striker you must try to get to the ball before your opponent. Frequently a defender will be favourite to get to the ball first but even then the striker must strive to get in front of the defender. Even if you arrive late you will make it difficult for the defender to play the ball away cleanly. A defender who knows that an opponent will always try to do this is constantly under pressure and worried.

A slogan for a striker might be: 'To get ahead, get in front'.

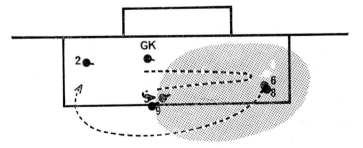

Fig. 23

Dribbling

In modern football the front players or strikers often find themselves receiving a pass when the nearest supporting attacker is a long distance away. The ability to hold the ball and 'screen' or 'hide' it from opponents is vital. At the same time it may be possible to use dribbling skill. In figure 24 the centre forward No. 9 has received a long clearance from his defence. He will be marked and challenged by an opponent and at least one opponent will move into a covering position. In this case No. 2 is moving to cover.

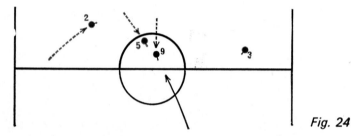

Fig. 24

In photo 20 the centre forward has screened the ball from his opponent and is trapping the ball with the inside of his foot and turning *at the same time.*

Before turning he will probably have feinted to give the impression that he intends to move the other way.

Photo 20   *Photo 21*   *Photo 22*

Photos 21 and 22 show this perfectly. If the striker can now make enough room to turn and face an opponent he should attack him with the ball. He should move towards an opponent and not away from him.

In the sequence in photos 23, 24, 25 and 26 we see the centre forward 'show' the ball to his opponent as if he is about to pass to a team-mate and then swivel away with the ball as the opponent tries to intercept the 'pass'.

Photo 23

Photo 24

Photo 25

Photo 26

In photos 27, 28 and 29 we can see another type of feint play. Here the centre forward has moved his right foot over the ball instead of playing it (notice how he has leaned to his left as if about to move in that direction). Then, having sent his opponent the wrong way, he has flicked the ball to his right. This is called 'selling a dummy'.

Photo 27   *Photo 28*   *Photo 29*

In photos 30, 31 and 32 the attacker has used a body swerve to send his opponent the wrong way. He has thrown his body and his weight to his left as if moving in that direction before pushing off his left foot in the opposite direction.

Occasionally an anxious opponent facing a striker will leave his legs too far apart in trying to establish a good challenging position. In photo 33 the attacker has accepted the invitation and pushed the ball through the opponent's legs.

Photo 30

Photo 31

Photo 32

Photo 33

Some attackers become very clever at drawing an opponent into a rash tackle by controlling the ball with the sole of their foot and, as the tackler lunges at the ball, the sole of the foot is used to pull the ball away.

One of the simplest methods of beating an opponent is to change your running speed, or 'change pace'as it is known. Never show an opponent your flat-out speed until you are sure it will result in a shot at goal. Develop the skill of running with the ball so that you are always changing pace and you have a small amount of extra pace when you need it. There are many relatively slow players who look much faster than they are because they can change pace smoothly and late.

Combined Play

However clever a striker is, he must look for help from other players to be really successful. Simple interpassing movements called 'one two's' are best. They are called 'one two's' because, generally speaking, only two passes are involved in getting past an opponent.

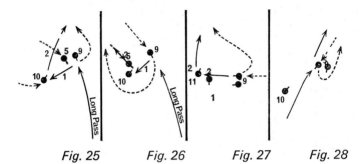

Fig. 25   *Fig. 26*   *Fig. 27*   *Fig. 28*

In figure 25 the centre forward No. 9 moves to receive a long pass from a defender. As the ball arrives he 'kills' the ball to No. 10 who gives a first-time pass behind the defender No. 5. The centre forward must kill the ball and turn sharply towards goal almost in the same movement.

In figure 26 from the same long clearance the centre forward has killed the ball and continued his run around the back of No. 10 to receive the second pass. Obviously the opposing No. 5 cannot follow him until he 're-appears' behind No. 10.

In figure 27 the striker No. 9 has run with the ball fairly close to a team-mate No. 11, who is marked. No. 9 gives a square pass and turns quickly to run behind both the opponents to receive the ball. This involves clever timing and acting since he must mime in such a way as to encourage No. 5 to follow him.

In figure 28, where the centre forward has moved to meet a firmly driven pass, there is the possibility of a 'one two' with No. 10. This time, however, No. 9 feints or pretends to kill the ball to his team-mate but deliberately misses the ball at the last moment and turns to follow it into space.

These simple interpassing movements require understanding and practice. That is what football skill is all about and practice certainly pays dividends.

Skill Practices
Shooting

In figure 29 two strikers, **A** and **B**, take up positions inside the penalty area preparing to receive serves from **C** and **D** alternately. The goalkeeper is in position and one defender, **X**. takes up a position within the GOAL AREA. **C** will serve by throwing or chipping the ball into the DROPPING ZONE and **B** will move to shoot. As soon as the ball has left the server's hands or foot, the defender **X** is allowed to 'come alive' and stop the striker shooting or getting in a successful shot. **B** has a number of choices.

    (a) Shoot first time.
    (b) Feint to shoot, perhaps dribble around the opponent **X** and then shoot.
    (c) Pass to partner **A** to shoot.

If he chooses (c) and passes to **A** then arrange the practice so that **A** *must* shoot first time. Fancy inter-passing inside the penalty area is not to be encouraged.

The next service comes from **D** to **A**, who has the same basic choices as his partner had.

If we ask **C** and **D** to deliver certain types of service we can make **A** and **B** practise methods of shooting. Very high services into the dropping zone will require **A** and **B** to head for goal and so on.

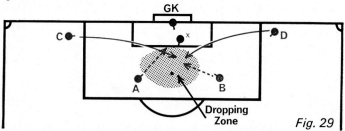

Fig. 29

In figure 30 player **A** takes up a position some 15 yards outside the penalty area with a server **Z** perhaps 5 or 10 yards behind him. The goalkeeper is in position while **X** and **Y**, who are defenders, together with **C** and **D**, who are attackers, take up positions outside the penalty area. **Z** serves to **A**, who must control the ball and move towards goal for a shot. Having served the ball, **Z** is also a defender who tries to recover to prevent a successful shot by **A**. As soon as the ball is served to **A**, **X** and **Y** can 'come alive' as defenders while **C** and **B** can offer themselves as passing possibilities to **A** if he cannot get in a shot. If **A** passes to **C** or **B** they must shoot first time. This practice is excellent for training players to make up their minds quickly in a shooting position.

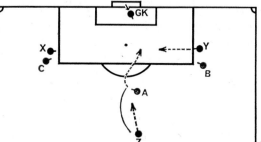

Fig. 30

3)

In figure 31 **A**, **B** and **C** are three attackers playing against two defenders, **X** and **Y**, together with a goalkeeper. Use these conditions:—

(1) The attackers must shoot within five passes.

(2) Only one pass can be made within the penalty area.

Small game practice of this kind is interesting and realistic if it is taken seriously. Players must not be allowed to take their time and 'fiddle' with the ball when they are in good shooting positions. Defenders will not allow you to do so in a match.

During shooting practice, particularly when you only have one ball, two ball 'catchers' behind the goal will ensure that practice is continuous.

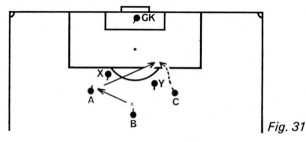

Fig. 31

Rapid Fire

Mark out a circle roughly thirty yards in diameter; for older players it should be rather more (figure 32). In the centre of this circle place three posts to make three goals rather smaller than full size goals, say 5 or 6 yards wide. The two goal-keepers have to defend all three goals. Six players are outside the circle and they have two footballs between them. The six attackers can interpass and shoot when they like FROM OUTSIDE THE CIRCLE. If they enter the circle they *must* try to dribble around the goalkeeper to score.

This practice will encourage quick snap shooting and it will also give the goalkeepers useful agility practice.

Fig. 32

Laying off Passes

The striker often receives the ball when he is facing his own goal. Sometimes he can control the ball and turn with it but, on many occasions, he will be wise to 'lay off' a pass to the feet of a team-mate who is facing the opponents' goal.

In figure 33 player **D** hits a long pass up to **A**, who is tightly marked by an opponent. The defending goalkeeper is in position. **A**, receiving the ball, MUST 'lay off' a first-time pass to either **C** or **B**, whichever is easier. In the diagram the passing sequence is numbered and **A** has laid his pass to **B**. **B** must now give a first-time pass to **C** or to **A**, who will move towards goal and try to score. If **A's** 'lay-off' pass is poor, **B** or **C** will have difficulty in playing a first-time pass. Perhaps you may have to relax the condition and allow **B** or **C** two touches in which to give a pass.

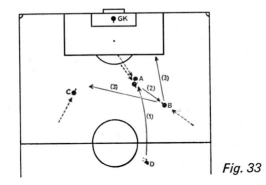

Fig. 33

In figure 34 the player **A**, while tightly marked by an opponent, will receive different services from **D**. **C** and **B**, who are supporting players, will play as follows: one will offer himself for a pass from **A** while the other will run through towards goal allowing **A** the possibility for sliding or glancing a pass behind the defender. In the diagram, **C** has decided to run forward to receive this kind of pass. Practice must never become mechanical and wherever possible the player receiving practice must be allowed a choice of action. Good footballers always have a choice, from two or three possibilities, of what to do.

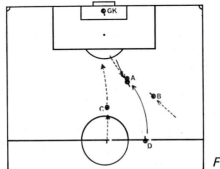

Fig. 34

Dribbling

Using the grid (figure 35), which is a series of squares, each square being 10 yards long and 10 yards wide, try the following practice. You can use as many squares as you have players. **A**, **B** and **C** are defenders who take up position at the back of their respective grid squares. As **X**, with the ball, moves into the first square from his starting position, **A** moves to stop him. **X** tries to dribble into the second square and if he is successful, **A** cannot challenge again. As soon as **X** arrives in the second square, **B** can move to challenge and so on up the ladder until **X** loses the ball or the ball leaves the ladder or until he successfully dribbles over the finishing line.

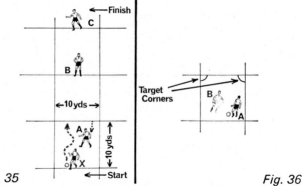

Fig. 35

Fig. 36

In figure 36, working in one square of the grid, player **A** tries to dribble past opponent **B**. All practice must have an aim and in this case **B**, the opponent, is trying to prevent **A** dribbling into the target corners without losing the ball or allowing the ball to be knocked out of the square. A bigger 'pitch', making the work harder, can be produced by working in two squares (the 'pitch' is now 20 yards long and 10 yards wide). The bigger the pitch used for dribbling practice the more a player can use speed, change of speed and stamina to beat his opponent. The smaller the pitch the more he must rely on cleverness and agility.

Taking Pace off the Ball and Turning

Strikers must be prepared to make the most of passes which are difficult to control. This particularly applies to central strikers or centre forwards if you like. On many occasions they will be challenged strongly while receiving the ball and when they are facing 'the wrong way' — this means their backs are pointing towards the opposing goal. An important skill involves 'laying off' passes to other players who are in a better position to go forward. Whenever he is given the smallest amount of space, however, the striker should be able to control the ball and turn to face his opponent in the same movement.

In figure 37 the central striker, No. 9, has managed to get away from the nearest opponent, No. 5. He has received a pass from red No. 4 and laid off a pass to red No. 8, who might give a pass for No. 11 to run for. The move has taken three passes and the ball has travelled perhaps 30 yards forward (4 to 9) and 10 yards backwards (9 to 8) before travelling 30 yards forward (8 to 11). The move has taken too much time, giving opponents a chance to position themselves to stop the move.

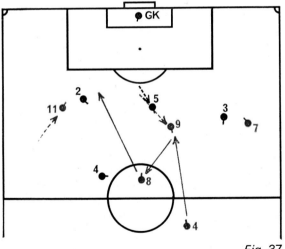

Fig. 37

In figure 38, No. 9 has received the pass from red No. 4, turning and controlling the ball at the same time. No. 9 is now in a position to do three things: he can pass to No. 11 (this pass is shorter and should be more accurate); he can pass to No. 7; OR he can attack the opposing No. 5 himself by dribbling. Two passes have caused trouble AND the ball has moved forward all the time. The opposing defenders are now in great difficulty. In photos 34, 35 and 36 we see a player preparing to receive a ground pass and turn in the same movement. In photo 34 the ball has arrived and the foot is pulled away or drawn back to take pace off the ball but NOT to stop it. This turning and controlling movement is carried on in photos 35 and 36.

Controlling and turning by taking the pace off a pass without actually stopping the ball is one of the key skills in modern football. The smaller the space in which you do this, the better player you will be. And remember all passes can be taken by any part of your body in the same way. Slow it down but don't stop it! In photo 37 we see the same idea used in controlling a waist high pass.

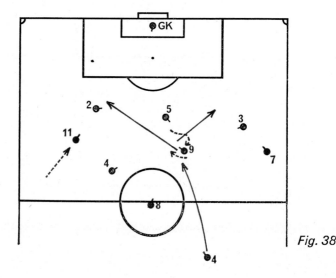

Fig. 38

Photo 34   Photo 35   

Photo 36

Photo 37

Heading

The greatest part of the striker's training and practice time will be given to shooting with BOTH feet and head. Strikers must LOVE to see the ball go into any goal; they must WANT to score, whatever the circumstances, more than anything else and they cannot get too much practice at it!

In figure 39 a winger (No. 7) with a number of footballs (one will do, of course) crosses the ball, aiming for areas **A** or **B**. Between them the two strikers will cover these two areas. At first perhaps No. 9 will always go for area **B** and No. 10 will go for area **A**. If the ball is aimed for area **B**, No. 9 will try to deflect the ball sideways into goal OR, if he is challenged by the goalkeeper quickly, he may try to deflect the ball with the top of his head towards area **A** and his team-mate, No. 10. No. 10 will then head for goal. If the ball is aimed for area **A**, No. 10 may be able to head for goal or he may have to head away from goal. In that case No. 9, having run into area **B**, must come out of goal to receive the header from his team-mate. If he doesn't he may find himself offside and so spoil a scoring chance.

Later, to confuse the goalkeeper and his defenders when they are there, 9 and 10 may practise cross-over runs where, by some pre-arranged signal, No. 10 runs to area **B** and No. 9 covers the far post cross at area **A**. As they improve, the strikers will want another defender in the practice to test their skill. If you ever want to test any new idea which you have practised, try it against one or two players who are acting as defenders.

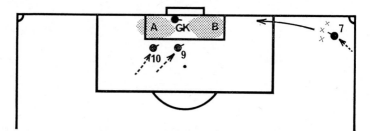

Fig. 39

Fitness Training
The striker must be capable of long periods of work (running, jumping and turning with and without the ball) and also periods of work when he has to move as fast as possible over short distances (10-30 yards).

Interval Training
In figure 40 player **A** starts on the penalty spot while players **B** and **C** stand outside the corner of the penalty area, each holding a ball. Player **D** is the time-keeper, holding a watch with a second hand or, better still, a stop watch. On the signal **A** runs towards **B** and the time-keeper starts his watch. The running pattern is as follows:

    A runs towards **B** and as soon as **A** has crossed the penalty area corner, **B** throws the ball gently to him. **A** controls the ball and passes back to **B**. **A** turns and runs to touch the penalty spot with one foot. He then runs towards **C** who, when **A** has crossed the corner of the penalty spot, serves the ball as **B** did. **A** controls the ball, passes back to **C** and turns back towards the penalty spot. **A** continues this pattern for exactly 60 seconds at which time **D** (the time-keeper) shouts 'Stop!'

Each trip from the penalty spot to receive a service counts 1. **A** tries to score as many points as he can in 60 seconds. The group of 4 then changes round quickly. The runner (in this case **A**) always becomes the time-keeper. **D** must take over from **B**, **B** takes over from **C** and **C** becomes the new runner. In this way each player is having one period of work (60 seconds) and three periods of rest (3 x 60 seconds = 180

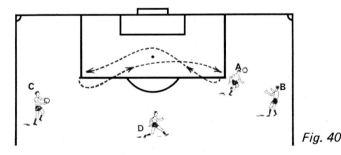

Fig. 40

seconds). To start with each player works 5 times with the rest in between and adds up his total score.

In figure 41 the same idea of work and rest is used. **A** starts in the restraining arc on the edge of the penalty area. When he enters the goal area **B** serves a ball and **A** shoots. (If he misses the goal he must fetch the ball himself.) Having shot, **A** turns, runs back to touch the ground *inside* the arc, turns again and heads towards the goal area and a serve from **C**. The drill is repeated for 60 seconds and the players change around.

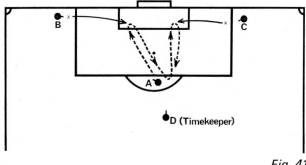

Fig. 41

Using the full pitch, if you have to train alone, the following pattern of training, using alternate spells of fast work, medium work and light work is used. (See figure 42.)

Starting at the half-way line the player jogs with the ball to point **A**. At **A** he picks up the ball and kicks it high into the penalty area; having kicked it, he sprints after it to shoot as quickly as possible **(B)**. The ball is retrieved and from point **C** the player kicks a high ball into the centre circle, sprints after it and tries to control the ball before it leaves the circle **(D)**.

A rest period follows since the player now walks around the centre circle. From **E** the ball is kicked into the penalty area for a following sprint and shot at goal **(F)**. The ball is retrieved and the player can walk slowly to **G**, at which point he dribbles the ball to the half-way line, imagining perhaps that he has to beat three or four opponents on the way.

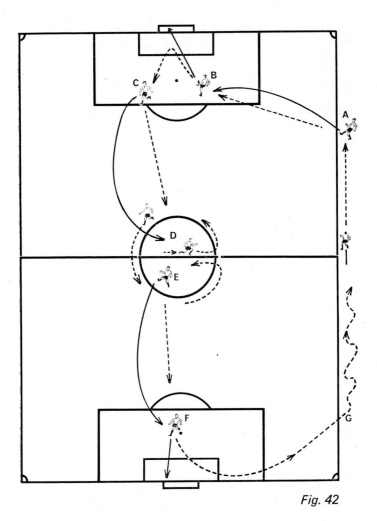

Fig. 42

157

Pressure Training

This form of training involves the running movements and techniques of the game and the fitness which is developed is directly related to the needs of football. Described simply, Pressure Training involves a controlled service of footballs to one player. As a result, the player must reproduce one or more football techniques in a situation which does not allow him to take his time in doing so. As he deals with one service he must change his position quickly to deal with another.

In figure 43 player **E** stands in the centre of a diamond formed by four players, **A, B, C** and **D,** each with a ball. In this practice we may require the striker to run and jump to head the ball back to another player. This is a technique frequently used by the central attacking players. **B** serves by throwing a high pass towards **E. E** runs, jumps and heads the ball back to **B**. As soon as he has headed the ball, he must turn and look for the next service from **C.** As he deals with that service he looks for a service from **D,** and so on in a clockwise direction around the diamond.

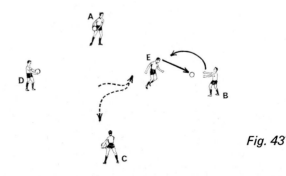

Fig. 43

Each player should work for 90 seconds and then change places with one of the players forming the diamond. In this basic Pressure Training situation any of the techniques of the game may be used. The service rate must be controlled in order to make the middle player work hard and, while working, he must try to produce high quality, accurate techniques.

In figure 44 the middle player **P** is surrounded by eight players. These players are in pairs, one with a football and one without. **A** has served the ball and this time **P,** the middle player, must control the ball with one touch before passing. As he controls it, any player without the ball may call for the pass. The servers always remain the same and the service moves in a clockwise direction from **A** to **B** to **C** and so on. This Pressure Training situation is varied to prevent the training attitude of **P** from becoming mechanical.

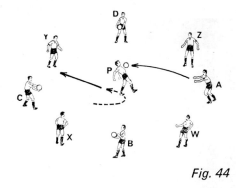

Fig. 44

In figure 45 the player under pressure, **(P)**, must produce different techniques. The service direction is from **E** to **A** to **B** and so on to **D**, and then in the OPPOSITE direction. **P** starts in the restraining arc on the edge of the penalty area. From **E's** service **P** tries to score. As soon as he has shot he runs to receive **A's** service, which he must pass first time back to **A**. From **B's** service he must head the return pass. From **C's** service he must control the ball and dribble it around **C** as quickly as he can; finally, from **D's** service he tries a shot. The service direction now moves in the opposite direction from **D** to **C** to **B** and so on back to **E**, when it changes again. The player behind the goal is there to retrieve the ball when **P** misses. This ensures a regular ball service which enables the pressure to be kept on **P**.

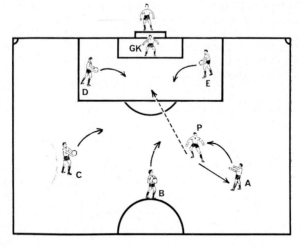

Fig. 45

Many Pressure Training situations can be organised with a little thought and imagination. Whatever form the training takes, remember that PRESSURE refers to a regular, unbroken and repeated service of one or a number of footballs. If the training situation is poor, too much time will be spent collecting mis-hit or mis-directed footballs and there will be no pressure on the player.

Central attackers must work hard in an unselfish way. Courage is important in enabling them to make goal scoring chances out of nothing. The striker, above all players, must be an optimist. Even if the side is losing heavily the good striker continues to search for any slight opportunity to pull the game back.